EXCELLING
IN LAW SCHOOL

*E*XCELLING IN LAW SCHOOL

A Complete Approach

Jason C. Miller
Attorney at Miller Johnson
in Grand Rapids, Michigan

Wolters Kluwer
Law & Business

Printed in the United States of America.

1 2 3 4 5 6 7 8 9 0

ISBN 978-0-7355-9924-6

Library of Congress Cataloging-in-Publication Data
Miller, Jason C., 1982-
    Excelling in law school : a complete approach / Jason C. Miller.
        p. cm.—(Academic success series)
    Includes index.
    ISBN-13: 978-0-7355-9924-6
    ISBN-10: 0-7355-9924-6
    1. Law—Study and teaching—United States. 2. Law—Vocational guidance—United States. I. Title.
    KF272.M53 2012
    340.071′173—dc23

                                                                            2012033803

About Wolters Kluwer Law & Business

Wolters Kluwer Law & Business is a leading global provider of intelligent information and digital solutions for legal and business professionals in key specialty areas, and respected educational resources for professors and law students. Wolters Kluwer Law & Business connects legal and business professionals as well as those in the education market with timely, specialized authoritative content and information-enabled solutions to support success through productivity, accuracy and mobility.

Serving customers worldwide, Wolters Kluwer Law & Business products include those under the Aspen Publishers, CCH, Kluwer Law International, Loislaw, Best Case, ftwilliam.com and MediRegs family of products.

CCH products have been a trusted resource since 1913, and are highly regarded resources for legal, securities, antitrust and trade regulation, government contracting, banking, pension, payroll, employment and labor, and healthcare reimbursement and compliance professionals.

Aspen Publishers products provide essential information to attorneys, business professionals and law students. Written by preeminent authorities, the product line offers analytical and practical information in a range of specialty practice areas from securities law and intellectual property to mergers and acquisitions and pension/benefits. Aspen's trusted legal education resources provide professors and students with high-quality, up-to-date and effective resources for successful instruction and study in all areas of the law.

Kluwer Law International products provide the global business community with reliable international legal information in English. Legal practitioners, corporate counsel and business executives around the world rely on Kluwer Law journals, looseleafs, books, and electronic products for comprehensive information in many areas of international legal practice.

Loislaw is a comprehensive online legal research product providing legal content to law firm practitioners of various specializations. Loislaw provides attorneys with the ability to quickly and efficiently find the necessary legal information they need, when and where they need it, by facilitating access to primary law as well as state-specific law, records, forms and treatises.

Best Case Solutions is the leading bankruptcy software product to the bankruptcy industry. It provides software and workflow tools to flawlessly streamline petition preparation and the electronic filing process, while timely incorporating ever-changing court requirements.

ftwilliam.com offers employee benefits professionals the highest quality plan documents (retirement, welfare and non-qualified) and government forms (5500/PBGC, 1099 and IRS) software at highly competitive prices.

MediRegs products provide integrated health care compliance content and software solutions for professionals in healthcare, higher education and life sciences, including professionals in accounting, law and consulting.

Wolters Kluwer Law & Business, a division of Wolters Kluwer, is headquartered in New York. Wolters Kluwer is a market-leading global information services company focused on professionals.

For

JEFFREY HOLST

Your initial difficulty and ultimate success taught me the value of having a good strategy and ensured that I had the necessary tools to excel in law school.

Contents

Acknowledgments

A BOOK LIKE THIS REQUIRES INPUT FROM A LOT OF OTHERS. I am grateful to all those who lent me their perspectives on the law school experience. I particularly want to thank Patrick Haney, Richard Marsh, Jared Haynie, William Wall, Clayton Kaiser, Dwayne Stresman, Jeff Wiggins, Jeffrey Holst, Jeff Hank, Hannah Murray, Luke Pelican, Jeremy Kidd, Steve Klein, Brad Glaza, and Sana Hamelin for their time and efforts. Without the help of my loving Karen, this book never would have been finished.

About the Author

JASON MILLER GRADUATED THIRD OUT OF A CLASS OF 410 STUDENTS from the University of Michigan Law School, where he was the managing editor of the *Michigan Telecommunications and Technology Law Review* and participated in a clinic and in moot court; he also worked while attending law school. He went on to clerk for the Honorable Deborah L. Cook of the United States Court of Appeals for the Sixth Circuit before joining the litigation department of Sherman & Howard, Denver's oldest law firm. In 2012 he relocated to Grand Rapids, Michigan, to join the law firm Miller Johnson.

A mediocre college student with an uninspiring LSAT score, Jason knew he would have to dramatically change his habits for law school, so he studied the strategies used by successful law students. Jason attended Ave Maria School of Law, a school ranked in the fourth tier by *U.S. News and World Report*; earned a 3.95 GPA; and was able to transfer to the University of Michigan, a top-ten law school, after his first year. At Michigan he continued to refine his successful strategies and ultimately graduated with a 3.97 GPA. In the course of attending two different law schools and interviewing people who attended many more, Jason developed an approach to help students identify the strategies that will work best for them.

Jason's writings have appeared in *St. John's Law Review, Southern Illinois University Law Journal, Criminal Justice, Seton Hall Circuit Review, Indiana Law Journal Supplement, Michigan Telecommunications and Technology Law Review, Journal of Technology Law and Policy, The Jury Expert, Public Corporation Law Quarterly, The Detroit News, Lansing State Journal,* and other publications.

Preface

LAW SCHOOL SUCCESS MEANS DIFFERENT THINGS TO DIFFERENT PEOPLE. To some, it is just a high GPA. To others, perhaps most students, it is all about getting "the job," and everything else is just a tool to achieve that. People land jobs in different ways. Some students get good grades—I call this the "prestige track"—while others build real-world skills. You might get disappointing grades with one plan and change course. This book is designed to help you get what you want out of law school. It covers academic topics such as getting good grades, but it also covers developing skills in clinical settings and working during law school. Hopefully you will find it helpful both as you pick what kind of success matters to you and as you strive to achieve that success.

There is no one right way to excel in law school—but there are many wrong ways, and this book should help to steer you away from those. This book is largely based on my own experiences as a student at two different law schools. I do, however, have my own quirky ways, so I discuss what others do and recommend, too. You have to find what works for you, and this book will help you do it.

This is a comprehensive book focused on strategy—not how classes *should* be graded but how they *are* graded and how you can excel. If it seems practical, pragmatic, blunt, and even possibly downright disrespectful, that's because it is. I tell you how things are and how you can deal with them within the system—this book is focused on the practical, not the principles. This book will not sugarcoat the truth about law school or life after law school. The legal job market can be very tough, which makes competition in law school even tougher.

The reality is that how you do in law school—and where you go to law school—makes a big difference in your job prospects upon graduation from law school and for at least the first few years after. The hiring Web site of Wheeler Trigg O'Donnell, a national litigation firm based out of Denver, expressly says what people at many other law firms think. The firm only hires attorneys who "have graduated from a top 10 law school or graduated in the top 10% of a top regional law school." The message is simple: If you are not coming out of a school like Harvard, you need to have good grades to be considered. And of course, even at Harvard, nothing is guaranteed these days. This book is designed to give you the edge you need to open the door to the opportunities you prize.

This is not a book about the law. It does not explain to you what you should learn in law school or the difference between courts of law and courts of equity. This is about tactics, not semantics. I will not give you an esoteric explanation of what it means to think like a lawyer. This book, though, is written with a lawyer's way of thinking.

Clients hire lawyers for one purpose: to identify the rules that govern their situations, and move their cases or structure their transactions in light of those rules. This book does exactly that, setting out the rules that govern processes like exam grading or law review selection and explaining how to work within those rules to get what you want. The message to take from this book is that you need to identify the laws or rules that govern what you want in law school, using either the general rules set out in this book or, preferably, specific rules that you get from your professors, and tailor your conduct to win within those rules in a way that works for you. That is how you excel in law school.

—Jason C. Miller

User Manual: Read This First

THIS BOOK IS DESIGNED TO HELP YOU DO WELL AT ALL STAGES OF LAW SCHOOL, from the rough first semester through making decisions about bar review at the end of your 3L year. As such, some topics—like getting on law review or publishing a paper as an upperclassman—will not make sense as a 1L or a 0L preparing to start law school. In the same vein, basic law school things will seem simple once you have already progressed within law school.

How to Use This Book

Because this book covers so many years of law school, it is not necessarily designed to be read cover to cover. I suggest using this book in two ways:

1. Read the sections that are relevant to you—e.g., the basics on how to take classes if you are about to start law school—and *skim* the sections about later law school things, such as picking upper-level paper topics. Skimming is a very important skill for lawyers to learn, and it will help you to know what is in the book for future use as topics come up.
2. Simply check the table of contents on pages ix-xii and read the sections that you need when you need them, coming back as needed throughout law school.

The chapters contain some repetition because you might not be reading them in a row. All books offering advice on law school and all commercial supplements are full of stuff you do not need. So is this book. You might be single, so you might skip the chapter offering advice for people in relationships in law school. Finding what you need and skipping what you do not is an important time-management skill in law school.

This is also a book that you should come back to. Highlight and mark up the advice or sections that seem best to you, but come back to it midsemester or after a semester and see if certain advice has new meaning or if an alternative strategy would be a good fit for you. Over time, I think you will find it quite helpful.

Voice

This book is based largely on my experiences attending two different law schools at opposite ends of the ranking and prestige spectrum. It is supplemented by research and advice from graduates and students of several other schools. I try to present what worked for me along with different strategies that worked for others. There is not just one right way to excel in law school.

You need to pick the strategies that work for you. This book is designed to equip you to do just that, which could sometimes mean doing the opposite of what I did. This book does not sugarcoat things. Law school is hard. The legal job market is harder. And the job market is even harder if you are at a less prestigious school given a lower ranking by *U.S. News and World Report*. This is not to say you are an inferior or bad person if you are not at Harvard, but the reality is that you face a different situation. I would not be doing you a favor by sugarcoating reality. But no *U.S. News* ranking will keep you from excelling in law school and getting a job if you work hard and smart.

EXCELLING
IN LAW SCHOOL

Chapter 1

INTRODUCTION

THIS CHAPTER IS DESIGNED TO GIVE YOU A PREVIEW of what you will face in law school and provide some information on decisions and choices you need (and do not need) to make before school starts. The first choice, of course, is whether to go to law school at all.

Whether to Go to Law School and Which Law School to Attend

Is Law School Right for You?

I recognize that you have already made your decision to attend law school and may not be interested in advice, but if you have not started law school yet, you should think seriously about your decision. The current legal job market is bad, and the number of law graduates is expected to outpace the number of new legal jobs for the foreseeable future. Law school is hard and expensive. Nobody should attend law school without looking at http://www.abovethelaw.com, a legal gossip blog that often reports on the tough state of the legal job market and the many legal professionals who regret their career path. Here's a great one-liner from the blog: "Given the state of the legal economy, getting minimum wage and health care to do actual legal work is a coup for a recent law grad in the Lost Generation."

My own particular advice is to go to law school only if you get into Harvard or a school in that caliber, receive a full scholarship, or can find fulfillment only by being a lawyer. This advice offends many, but hopefully it prompts you to ask yourself why you are going to law school. There are many good reasons to go, but also many bad reasons. Going to law school is a serious decision, and you should not go to law school just because you have not found a better option.

Some Quick Thoughts on Where to Go

Where to go can be a very tough decision. For personal or family reasons, some students are limited in where they can go, but many students have options. The clichéd advice is to go to a school that is in or near the legal market you want to practice in. There are a handful of truly national schools, such as Harvard, that are often referred to as the T14—the same 14 schools have rotated around the top of the *U.S. News & World Report* rankings for years. But most schools place most of their graduates in and have the strongest alumni network in the region where the school is located. If you want to practice in a particular state, it may be better to go to school there than to attend a university in another state. There are some exceptions to this rule, but it is helpful to keep it in mind. Research the school before you go. And do not rely solely on the school's own marketing materials and Web site. The school has a strong incentive to get you to pay them all those tuition dollars, and some schools are even being sued for putting allegedly deceptive information about job prospects on their Web sites. Do your homework before enrolling in a school.

Many students face a trade-off between the prestige of the school and financial aid money. Many law schools are focused on the metrics that boost their ranking with *U.S. News*—particularly undergrad GPA and LSAT scores. To boost their rankings, many schools give scholarships to students whose GPA or LSAT numbers are substantially higher than the school's median. The basic rule is that you might be able to get a full or partial scholarship by attending a school substantially less prestigious than the highest-ranked school you can get into. This is a very important decision to make. This book does contain a section on getting scholarships in law school, but the single best opportunity to get big scholarship money is in deciding where to go to law school.

What to Expect in Law School: The Basics

If you have not started law school yet and do not know any law students or graduates, the whole process may seem bewildering. Having some understanding of what to expect in law school might help you to prepare for the experience to come. In addition to the slew of books about law school, there are a few popular movies. Set at Harvard, *The Paper Chase* (1973) is considered the classic movie about the stress of the first year of law school, but you shouldn't let that one scare you. Even the more recent comedy *Legally Blonde* (2001), also set at Harvard, might have some value in showing how stressful the first day of law school can be and in its representation of Socratic dialogue in the classroom. Reading this book, talking to law students, and even watching movies can give you an idea of what you will face, but a quick summary up-front might be helpful.

To state the obvious, law school is very different from an undergraduate program. You must study a lot more and much harder. You are usually graded on a true curve against your peers, which means you have to do better than others to earn top grades. Most students' law school grades are lower than their undergraduate grades, which can come as a shock to those with a history of excellent marks. Generally, your entire grade for the class will be decided by a difficult final exam.

Law school classes are usually conducted through Socratic dialogue, which means that professors might call on you out of the blue to answer questions. And at the same time that you are studying hard for classes, you must also spend time looking for jobs to gain legal experience. If all goes according to plan, you will likely work some kind of job during the summers between your first and second years and between your second and third. Law school requires a great deal of focus, energy, work, and juggling. Combine these with solid strategies for success, and you can ace it.

Staying Healthy in Law School

The importance of maintaining your health in law school should be fairly obvious. A healthy body and healthy mind are necessary to support the kind of focus and analysis you'll do in law school. It's one of the best tips anyone can offer for performing well on exams. The simplest step is to make sure you get the right amount of sleep. Be realistic in your sleep needs. While some people can get by with only a few hours, most of us require a full night's rest. It is especially important to be realistic about your sleep needs going into exams. Law school exams don't test rote memorization—they test analytical thinking. While you can cram vocabulary terms to ace some undergraduate exams, law school requires a sharp mind to spot and understand issues learned over time.

Keep up your immune system over the course of a semester so that illness doesn't bog you down or impede your studies—even if it's as simple as taking a multivitamin. You should also find time to exercise. If you don't think you have time to maintain your pre-law-school exercise regimen, try to find ways to adapt. Get lectures on MP3 (Kaplan PMBR has an excellent set for first-year classes, and some free podcasts are available from the Center for Computer-Assisted Legal Instruction [CALI]) and listen to them while at the gym, or review flashcards while on an exercise bike. My 1L roommate could not find time for the gym, so he took a few minutes to do push-ups and pull-ups in the library every day. While strange, it was effective. Finally, watch your alcohol consumption and the temptation to self-medicate to deal with law school problems—the legal profession is particularly susceptible to substance abuse.

What to Do Before Law School

There are many different answers to this question. Some will tell you to just have fun, because law school will be so intense. One person told me to do lots of pleasure reading in the months before law school because it would give me practice for the high volume of reading I would have to do in law school—and because most law students simply don't find the time for pleasure reading.

If you're reading this book before starting law school, it seems that you've already opted for a more intense route. In addition to reading this, you can try to prepare for a class before it starts, such as forcing yourself to quickly read through outlines or commercial supplements and briefly reading up on your professors. I gave one law student Kaplan PMBR's 1L review MP3s to listen to the summer before he started law school. He listened to them—several hours for each class—during his commute to work, and he listened to the more interesting subjects (for instance, criminal law and constitutional law) more than once. While he obviously couldn't master the material during this time, he reported that learning it later during law school seemed much easier for him than for his peers because the concepts and terms were not entirely new to him at that point. If you're a real overachiever, you can also try to do things that you will not have time to do in law school, like reading material your professors have written.

While this kind of effort can give you a jump-start on law school, it's not critical for your success, and you can feel free to avoid the extra labor before you make the transition to the intensities of law school if you wish.

Pre-Law-School Logistics: What to Take Care of Before Classes Start

Law school has a much more intense start than college. Even those who have been in the work force for years may be used to a longer orientation or training period when starting a new job. (Working a job in law school is covered in Chapter 13). And while your school will undoubtedly have an orientation program, your classes will likely have required reading before the first day. Your first week of class will require you to read dozens or possibly hundreds of pages of text. To make the first week even more difficult, often the first cases you read as a 1L are old cases written in archaic language. To the extent you can take care of anything in your life before being thrown into the fire of law school, you should do so.

Where to Live

Of course you will figure out where to live before starting school, but make sure you think it through rather than accepting a housing decision on default. Thinking things through ahead of time is a theme you will find repeated constantly in this book, and it is no less important in deciding where to live. In terms of geography, find a place where you feel comfortable. Some students want to live a little farther from campus, where things may be quieter and cheaper. My top suggestion here is to avoid long commutes. One of my good friends had an hour-and-fifteen-minute commute each way during his 1L year. That year he got Cs. The next two years he cut the commute down to 15 minutes and got As. Avoid long commutes.

If you are going to rent, like most law students, living alone has its obvious advantages and creates a quiet environment. It also tends to cost more money, and the more debt you take on during school, the more difficult life is after law school and the fewer career choices you may have. Living with other law students means that your roommates will share the experience with you. They will understand what is going on with exams and the stress in your life. They can also bring law school drama into your home and prevent you from being able to escape law school when you are done for the night. Roommates who aren't law students give you the chance to spend time with people who do not eat, sleep, and breathe law school. Some find this refreshing. At the same time, those roommates will not understand just how hard law school is or how crazy exam time is for you. Carefully consider your options.

Another option to consider is the length of your lease term. You may want to try for an academic-year lease rather than a one-year lease. Being free of your lease when the school year ends provides you with the option to go somewhere else for summer employment. In this new economy, flexibility matters, and the ability to go wherever you need to in order to get the experience might be worth negotiating a shorter lease.

Technology

Most students use laptops in class. But it's a good idea to make sure you have a reliable laptop in place when school starts. You do not need to buy a new laptop just to take notes, but make sure you have something reliable that will not die on you. At most schools students take final exams on laptops, too, and you do not want to add nervousness and stress about your computer dying to the high-stress exam week. Wait to decide on other expensive items, such as e-readers, until you figure out if you need such products.

Picking Classes

First-year students usually do not have a choice in what classes they take, so you do not have to stress about this when school starts. You will likely be assigned to a section and will take all of your classes with students from that section.

Getting a Concentration

Typically, all law students simply get a juris doctorate (JD). Many schools now offer various concentration or certificate programs, from trial advocacy to intellectual property. To earn this extra credential, which theoretically makes you more specialized, you have to take a certain grouping of classes. A concentration, though, is only worth pursuing if you really want to be specialized. If you are completely sure you want to be a tax attorney, then go for the tax program, but if you are unsure about your future or about whether there is a future in a particular field (for instance, whether you can make a living in International Human Rights), go for the general degree. This is something you can research before starting school, but it's not something you will have to decide before the first day.

Managing Your Finances

Law school debt can be crushing. There is an entire genre of blogs in which law school graduates complain about how they cannot repay the loans or how their lives have been ruined by loans. Being responsible with your finances can only be a good thing; being irresponsible can limit your career choices—it is difficult to take a $35,000-per-year public defender job when you have $200,000 in debt. You may have little control over tuition prices, but you do have control over how you spend your own money or excess loan money.

At a basic level, you need to spend like a student and not a lawyer. Live like a student now so you do not have to live like a student after law school. You will undoubtedly see some classmates leasing nicer vehicles and taking expensive vacations. Some are doing this with family money, but others are going into debt for it. Do not fall into this trap. Earning money in law school is discussed in Chapter 13 and getting scholarships is covered in Chapter 12. As a starting point in school, though, you can just try to manage spending, which is easier than trying to earn money while studying for exams and looking for summer law jobs.

Plan the Work, Work the Plan, Evaluate the Plan, and Adapt the Plan: A General Approach to Law School

Developing a strategy and finding a routine that works is essential for law school success. You need to be open-minded in your approach to law school and accept that you do not know what you do not know. Law school is different from undergrad, which you know, but that means that the strategies that got you into law school might not help you excel in law school.

Going into law school, you will not know exactly what will work for you. You have to be willing to allow yourself to change tactics regularly while you find out what works for you. This does not mean that you should change course on a whim. Put together a plan for the semester based on the strategies discussed in this book, the things that worked for you in the past, and the things that you think will work for you in the future. Make a conscious effort to evaluate what is working and what is not. Talk to others about what they are doing and see if it makes sense for you—do not do something just because everyone else is. Reevaluating your strategies mid-semester may be appropriate if you are having real trouble, but in general set aside some mental time at the end of each semester to think about what worked and what did not. You do not want to end up in your third year barely figuring out what you did wrong the first two years. Keep fine-tuning your routine until it works.

This approach will also keep you focused on school and strategy. Focus is the mental goal. You do not want to be too anxious. The confidence that comes from having a plan can help avoid that. But you also do not want to be overly confident. The ideal mental state for law school is probably slightly concerned but without any panic. Building a solid routine should help that. It will also help you to focus on school and avoid distractions.

Law school is a professional school. Unless you are going to law school for a strange reason, you chose this path because you wanted to excel in law school and get a job with your JD. This means you are there to learn, do well, and get a job, not to make friends. I am not suggesting you be antisocial. Friendships and relationships are important, and making friends with other students and attorneys is good for your career, but you need to have a serious approach and focus on the end result. Striking a balance between friends and academics is key, but do not think of law school as primarily a social experience. The chapters that follow explain how to focus on and succeed in all aspects of law school.

Key Points

- Analyze your reasons for going to law school and carefully decide whether or not attending is right for you.
- Be careful and particular about where you go to law school; your choice should take into account what kind of law you want to practice, what level of prestige you want to have in your practice, and where you want to practice.
- Deciding which school to attend will offer you your most significant and easiest opportunity for huge savings in the form of scholarships.
- The general trend is that you are likely to receive more scholarship offers from less prestigious schools than from more prestigious schools.
- Take care of your life issues *before* law school begins, and if you can, try to get a head start in your reading and studying.

- Be mindful and respectful of your body's abilities and limitations; stay hydrated, stay healthy, and get enough sleep. Law school exams require critical thinking and analysis that is difficult or impossible to accomplish when you're under the weather and exhausted.
- Financially speaking, live like a student now so you don't have to live like a student after law school. Excessive debt can even limit the types of jobs you can afford to take when you graduate.
- Practice continual self-improvement by modifying your approach and strategies to studying throughout your tenure in law school.

Chapter 2

FAMILY AND THE LAW SCHOOL EXPERIENCE

AT THE OUTSET, IT IS IMPORTANT TO REALIZE THAT YOUR PARTNER must be committed to your becoming a lawyer. If he or she isn't, then you should reconsider law school. Most married students I talked to said their partners intuitively understood the demands of law school and how necessary the hours of studying are. Nevertheless, it might be beneficial to make sure your partner understands exactly the kind of workload you face and how important these three years are for your career. You are sacrificing today to reap the benefits tomorrow. Even with an understanding partner, going through law school with a spouse or children, or both, requires special consideration and strategies.

Boundaries

Setting boundaries is extremely important when you have someone else who can make legitimate and serious demands on your time. There are many different ways to set boundaries. One particularly driven student I know decided to set a limit on how late he would study and negotiated a cut-off time with his wife. He wanted to study from the early morning until 8:00 P.M., but they eventually agreed on 6:00 P.M. as the cut-off. He also never studied on Sundays, reserving this for family time. Another friend blocked out family time from 5:00 P.M. to 8:00 P.M. and limited weekend studying to exam time, with a special emphasis on eating dinner together and making the most of the designated family time. You will have to determine when you study best, how much time you need, and how much time your family needs from you. While you need to have a plan established up front, you really do not know what law school is like until you are in it, so it would be best to plan on revisiting the boundaries at least once a month for the first semester, if not the first year, in order to make sure the needs of both you and your family are met.

Another married student studied heavily only around exam times and established that his partner could briefly visit during these daylong marathon sessions so that they could eat together but would have to leave immediately after the meal. Yet another student set one night each week to stay at the library until midnight to free up time on other days, making a special effort to maximize the work done that night. Set whatever boundaries are necessary to support your study style, ask your partner to approve them, and stay within them. When your partner knows that he or she can count on you to honor those boundaries and not study during family time, it will be easier for your partner to let you work to the full extent you both agreed upon. Boundaries can be even more important during finals, as there is a great temptation to just let everything go save studying, but this is all the more reason to set specific boundaries that cover your finals period.

Married students might also consider setting a boundary concerning exam grades. Law students will quickly find that professors' conscientiousness in grading exams and providing grades to the administration for approval and release varies greatly, from diligent to dilatory. It is not uncommon for a final exam (which constitutes a student's only graded exercise for the entire term) to be given in mid-December but for grades to come out in early February. Although most students avoid discussing postexam performance with their peers, you'll find it impossible to avoid talking about it with your partner, who will be dying to know how you think you did. As a 1L, you will not have any idea how you did on the exams, so your grade speculation and fear of bombing your classes is truly just speculation. Your partner might want to talk to you about the exam on the day of, but he or she may *not* be interested in hearing your speculation, depression, and obsession with grades during the six weeks of waiting. On the other hand, you might not want to talk about your grades, knowing that it would just be speculation, but your partner could be dying to know how you did. This is another reason that setting expectations and boundaries ahead of schedule is important, because your partner needs to understand what you are comfortable talking about. If you do not discuss your exams, your partner may begin to think that you are withdrawing from the family, which can lead to conflict.

Strategies

Meeting the demands of a partner or children requires some extra planning to make sure you use your time efficiently and study at the agreed-upon times. Here are some tips others have shared with me.

Leaving Home to Study

Many married students, especially parents, report having to leave the house to get work done. Leaving home to study for the day can actually be difficult and sorrowful, especially if you have kids, but you might have to find a way to do it. Stick within a set of healthy boundaries to reassure yourself. It might not be wise to change your routine too dramatically during finals. Some married students try to get away from their family during finals (checking into a hotel room or sending their partner on a trip), but the lack of distractions might not compensate for the loneliness, lack of companionship, and disruption in your routine. Think this one over before you distance yourself at exam time. After facing a particularly bad 1L exam, it might be more comforting to have your partner around than to have the extra free time to move on to the next exam topic.

Timing

Planning your study time can help your relationship. Parents might want to plan a study routine around their kid's sleeping habits. You might try to study when your partner is at work or around his or her social schedule—if he or she is in a Wednesday evening bowling league, plan on studying Wednesday evenings. Small children present a special set of challenges, as sleep is almost always an issue for their parents. Avoid needing to cram around exam times by working early, often, and in manageable blocks.

For some, getting up early to study is much more effective than trying to study after a full day of school followed by evening family obligations. Maximizing the return on your time really matters, and the sooner you figure out how to do this, the better. Rather than stumbling into a rhythm over the course of a few years of law school, try to think about what works for you in the circumstances you face, and then plan to reevaluate your routine in a month. Keep fine-tuning your routine until it works.

Social Life

As a married law student, you face the difficult task of balancing your home life with an academic program that takes up the entirety of many students' time. You only have so much social time, and one way some achieve balance is by limiting their social schedules to things involving their partners—in other words, they do not hang out with their friends without inviting their partners. Others, though, recognize that their partners would rather avoid hearing know-it-all 1Ls parroting Law and Economics concepts, and leave their partners at home when hanging out with other students. Once again, this may be a good area to set boundaries in. Also, look for any social activities your school or its clubs put on for students with partners and children and take advantage of them.

Encouraging Your Partner to Take Advantage of the "Lost Time"

One very successful married student (without children) encouraged his wife to take advantage of the "lost time." She was a Division I collegiate swimmer and had been out of school for around three years when he started law school. She missed the competition and friendship of her competitive swimming days, and she took advantage of the massive amounts of time her husband was devoting to law school to renew her passion. She joined a local triathlon club and began training for triathlons, first for a hobby and then as an intense, top-flight competitor. Her success was atypical, but if your partner has an interest—learning Spanish, taking guitar lessons, whatever it may be—this may be the time to encourage him or her to pursue it as a way of occupying his or her time when you are busy studying.

Explaining the Law

Some students like to talk to their partners about what they are learning. They find value in having their significant others feel included in what they are doing. The value for your studies comes in what you learn by verbalizing it. As you try to explain something from class, listen for any inconsistencies or things that just do not make sense. I found this exercise helpful, both for learning the material and for developing stronger relationships with my father and girlfriend (we got married after law school). I spent time trying to teach them about the interesting things from torts or criminal procedure and kept the details of antitrust law's "small but significant and nontransitory increase in price" (SSNIP) test to myself. Not everyone has the time for or interest in this kind of intellectual discussion. If your partner is not interested in listening to you talk about the material, do not be offended, but take advantage of his or her interest if possible.

Chapter 3

Preparing for and Participating in Class

Introduction to Class

LAW SCHOOL CLASSES ARE DIFFICULT. Many are taught in a traditional Socratic method. The professor calls on students to discuss facts and points of law. Rather than lecturing the student on the answer, the professor may ask questions designed to elicit the answer from the student. When you are the student "in the hot seat" and are actually being called on by the professor, it can be nerve-wracking. But even when you are sitting in the audience, it can be difficult—it's hard to take notes when you're not sure if the student is giving the right answer.

Rather than reading a typical undergraduate textbook that tells you the information you are supposed to learn and may even put the really important details in bold, law students are usually forced to read casebooks. These massive books contain edited cases arranged to cover a topic. You are supposed to read the case and figure out *why* you were supposed to read the case. Sometimes this is quite easy—the rule of law you are supposed to learn is very clearly discussed and articulated. Sometimes, though, you are forced to read old but important cases written in arcane language that still leave you scratching your head after several read-throughs. This is why you need a strategy to prepare for and participate in class.

How Class Participation Affects Your Grade

Earlier I explained that the final exam is the most important part of your law school grade and that spending too much time on other things can distract you from preparing for your exams. But class participation can affect your grade a little bit, and you should plan on using this to your advantage. Most professors will alter your grade by up to one-third (e.g., moving a B to a B+) based on class participation. While it seems possible that a particularly poor performance in class could lower you grade by one-third, it is most likely that your participation will either not affect your grade or move it up by one-third. This section focuses on how to get that one-third participation boost.

You should always try for the participation boost. If your goal is to ace your classes, being able to count on the participation boost means that you might be able to land an A— on the exam and still pull a full A in the class. If your goal is just to survive your classes, the principle is equally applicable. Generally, participation will not give you a full letter grade boost, so spending too much time focusing on this area can be a waste. As with all things in law school, you must strike a balance. A participation boost is comparatively easy to get—the studying required to move your grade on an exam from an A— to an A takes much more effort than the participation required to have the same effect—and should always be worked for.

Exactly how professors decide to give a participation boost will always be something of a mystery and varies from professor to professor. Some professors are better organized than others. One professor I had kept the seating chart with him at all times and put checks next to a student's name every time he or she participated and said something intelligent. At the end of the semester, those with the most check marks received the boost. Many professors are less formal than that. For some it is an opportunity to play favorites and adjust the final grades. Others make sure participation is kept separate from exam grading. One of my professors actually handed his secretary a separate list of students who had participated enough to receive a discretionary boost and had the secretary adjust the final grades accordingly, without the professor ever having seen the final grades. Following the advice outlined in this section, though, should help you succeed no matter how your professor monitors and considers performance.

How to Read and (Maybe) Brief Cases and Casebooks to Prepare for Class

When you start law school, you should brief cases. As a first-year student, you will probably hear a lot from other students about briefing cases. The emphasis some students place may unnerve you and the term itself may be confusing. A case brief for a first-year is different from the kinds of briefs (actual legal filings) that lawyers and upper-level students talk about. A case brief is an aid that helps you identify and organize what you need to know to be able to discuss the case effectively in class. A good case brief should cover the essential facts of the case, the lower court holding, the procedural posture (how this case came to the appellate court), the issue for the court to decide, the rule of law produced by the court in this case, and the result (who won the case). These are the essential pieces of information to know and have at your fingertips so that you can discuss the case if called on. However, it's important to remember that you are not graded on your case briefs.

Every minute you spend briefing cases for class is a minute you did not spend preparing for your exams, which are the basis for your grade. You need to turn from briefing cases to studying for exams as soon as you can. This is a weaning process. At first you will need to spend a lot of time reading cases and writing up case briefs to help you understand what happened in a court case and develop the skill of pulling out the material that your professor wants. But after you teach yourself to read cases, you should stop spending the extra time writing out briefs. Here is my three-step process to develop the ability to read cases.

Step One

First, you need to actually do case briefs. Whether you write them out on your computer or write them by hand on a legal pad, you should put down a summary of the key facts as noted above. It may be difficult at first to spot the procedural posture or to identify which facts are relevant (such as who made the initial offer in a contracts case) and which facts can be ignored (such as where the defendant was incorporated in a contracts case). Forcing yourself to hunt for this information and write it down will help you to develop the ability first to find that information more quickly and then to realize what is pertinent after you read it the first time. You may have to read a case multiple times, or at least read it once and skim it multiple times, to be able to find the information to fill out your case brief. Continue briefing through the second step, outlined below, and stop as you are ready to move on to the third step.

Step Two

The second step is to spend the first few weeks of law school reading every case twice. On your first read-through of the case, just force yourself to get through it. You are reading not necessarily to comprehend but just to get through it and to see where the case is going. Do not worry about underlining or highlighting this time, just push yourself through it and have faith that you will understand the case on your second read-through. Make this read-through quick and direct, but do not skim. After forcing yourself to push on through the case, go back later (you can do this immediately afterward or within a day or two) and read the case for comprehension. This time try to understand the case; try to spot the key facts and the ruling. Mark up your case by highlighting or underlining the important information or writing in the margins. Some students color-code their highlighting, using different colors to indicate the facts, law, and procedural posture. If you are a visual, color-oriented person this might work for you. It always seemed to me that students who did this spent too much time worrying about which color to use. I typically used a blue pen so my marks stood out from the black writing. I underlined key information or important-sounding quotes in the text of the case and wrote little notes in the margin next to the information (like "facts:"; "holding:"; or "P loses") to make it easy to find. Experiment with different styles to see what works best for you while reading to comprehend, and once you've found a method of marking up your cases, stick with it. As you become more comfortable with this method you can stop reading a case twice and stop briefing it. Some students might be ready to make this transition in the first few weeks of law school; others may take several weeks. But at some point you need to force yourself to stop briefing cases and reading cases twice because you need the time to prepare for exams to ace law school.

Step Three

The third step is to begin book briefing your cases—that is, to rely on your notes in your book rather than writing out a separate brief to prepare yourself for class. Now that you've sufficiently marked up your casebook and identified the information you need on the page, you can use the casebook itself if you are called on by your professor. You will be reading a lot of cases during your first year, and it is hard to keep them separate. At the top of the case, write a short summary of the case to refresh your memory—something like "man who goes in backroom to get boxes becomes licensee, not invitee," or something even shorter if you develop your own shorthand or can capture the main idea and facts more succinctly. Read for class during your regular personal study time and mark up the cases (book briefing) to help you in class. Prior to every class, spend just a few minutes flipping through your casebook and looking at your summaries at the tops of the cases, and note where in the case you indicated the facts or other key information is. This will help you to remember the topic of the case and to find the information quickly if called upon.

A key part of this third step is to practice continual self-improvement. Pay attention to what your professor likes. Is your professor always interested in the procedural posture of a case? Does your professor care about the standard of review? Does your professor like to discuss the jurisprudential theories in the dissent, or does your professor never discuss or mention a dissent? Your goal, in addition to actually understanding the case, is to mark up the information in your casebook that corresponds to the questions your professor is going to ask. If your professor asks something that draws on information or a quote in the case that you had not identified or marked up, then mark it up in class and make a mental note that you failed to recognize its significance. Keep learning what your professor wants and adjust the information you underline or highlight in your casebook accordingly. Almost all casebooks include short notes after the main case. These may include the editors' comments on the case, short summaries of other cases, or hypothetical questions. Reading the notes after the cases is often the best thing you can do to prepare for exams and class discussion. These notes are written by other professors, and your professor may take advantage of them. Read these notes before class and see if your professor draws on the concepts in class. Eventually, you might get good enough to know exactly what your professor wants you to get out of a case, but the way to do this is to recognize what you've missed.

Striking the Balance

This three-step process is my method for striking the appropriate balance in preparing for class. This balance is important because class participation affects your grade, you don't want to sound stupid, and class has at least some bearing on your exams. However, preparing for class is different from preparing for exams, and you do not want preparing for classes to eat up too much of your time when you could be learning how to apply the law to facts as you need to be able to for your exams. There are other ways to strike this balance.

One friend, recognizing that he was graded based on his exams, not on class, decided not to read for class at all. Aspen publishes a series called Casenote Legal Briefs. These commercial case briefs provide case summaries and the details you need to know for class. The case briefs are "keyed" to your specific textbook. Other companies also provide commercial case briefs, but I have never seen anybody use them and cannot comment on their quality. My friend read the Casenote Legal Briefs just before class and then had them open in class. This is a risky choice. He did not participate well in class, ran the risk of being asked a question not covered in the case brief, and did not receive a discretionary participation boost in his grade from the professor. However, he was able to devote all his study time to exam prep—even early in the semester—and he did extremely well in law school. It's too risky a strategy for me, though. Commercial case briefs are better used in conjunction with the actual cases, rather than as a substitute.

Another friend used a slacker method to prepare for class. She would read—or, more accurately, skim—the casebook in preparation for class and then read the commercial case briefs. She would have both the case briefs and the book open in class but spent very little time reading cases for class. It's less risky than not reading but not as solid as my method. My suggested approach for those using Casenote Legal Briefs is to read the brief first, then read the actual case, then bring both to class. Reading the brief before the case will make the case easier to digest and point you toward the right information while still giving you a chance to get the feel of the case itself.

Some students do not realize the need to strike a balance at all. They brief cases throughout their first year, or at least until the end of their first semester, and then realize in the week before exams that they have plenty of .doc files on their computer that tell them the facts and history of cases, but they do not understand how to spot issues on law exams or apply the law to a new set of facts. Do not fall into this trap. When you begin to read your casebook, do so with the end goal in mind: You want to develop the ability to get the most out of the book in the least amount of time so that you can use the time saved to prepare for exams.

Note-taking

Law school classes are different from other classes and present a unique challenge in note-taking. The case method means that a big chunk of the information flying around in a class deals with facts and details, not necessarily law and analysis that you need to know. A Socratic dialogue means that much of the talking will be done by students, some of whom will give inarticulate or even outright wrong answers. You should approach note-taking with the same strategic, goal-oriented focus that you approach any other aspect of law school. You should take notes to help you perform well on exams and to help you with a potential class participation grade boost.

If you read (and maybe brief) for classes, prepare to answer questions in class, and prepare for exams with the methods discussed earlier, it might seem like your class notes accomplish little. But taking class notes helps you to capture your professor's specific view on a topic, identify areas where your personal intuition and the actual law conflict, stay engaged in class, and develop your own outline if you decide to do so.

Your professors are obviously a great resource when you're preparing for final exams. You should note where your professor disagrees with cases or with the case-book editors. If your professor has a particular slant, note that. For example, if your criminal procedure professor thinks that modern courts are conservative and that defendants always lose due to either broad application of harmless error or strong deference to lower courts that always trust the cop over the criminal, this should make it into your notes. Your professor might have a succinct way of explaining something or his or her own "test" that is derived from the precedent. This kind of information will actually help you learn the material better, not just give an answer the professor wants.

With any area of the law, you will have a guess as to the outcome. When asked whether a person can use deadly force to defend his or her property, you probably have an intuitive answer and even have some guess as to why. On many issues your intuition will be right; on some it will be wrong. Identifying and focusing on the areas where your gut instinct does not match up with the law is a key aspect of learning the law and doing well. You can retrain your instincts by taking more, and more emphatic, notes on topics where your instinct is just plain wrong. If the professor asks a student a question about the law or the application of the law, always try to venture a guess in your own mind. If your guess was wrong, then pay close attention to the ensuing discussion and make sure you capture what you need to capture in your notes to retrain your instincts.

How to Take Notes

Many students have difficulty paying attention in class. You won't have this problem during your first few days of law school. But as the days (and years) wind on, many students' minds drift due to distractions—especially those who surf the Web during class. Taking notes is a way to force yourself to pay attention. Many of your professors do notice if you're looking at your computer screen and typing at a throttle that matches the pace of class discussion or staring intently at the screen and clicking every so often with an intensity that suggests you're browsing blogs or shopping for shoes, even if they don't call you out for it. This is not to say that your professors want you to just type away. They want you to pay attention and participate. For some, typing intensely is a tool that forces them to pay attention; for you, it may be a distraction. In fact, some professors have banned note-taking or assigned a rotation where one or two students take notes on any given day so that others are free to participate in class.

Taking notes can help you to participate and interact by giving you notes on the discussion to refer to in later class discussion or with the professor outside of class. You might be able to note your questions on the material or any of the professor's questions that stumped you. Whatever reason you choose to take notes, be strategic about it. A stream-of-consciousness set of notes that records every mind-numbing student answer will not be helpful for later review, and that level of intensity in note-taking will probably end up distracting you from participating in class. If you are going to prepare your own outlines, your class notes will be your primary tool. Taking good, concise notes without too much student gibberish will save you a lot of work when you start the arduous process of converting your notes into an outline.

Today, almost all professors permit students to use laptop computers and almost all students choose to use laptop computers. Some students do insist on taking notes by hand. Some antitechnology types are scared of their computers crashing, others insist they learn better by writing by hand, and still others feel that the pen and paper free them from the distractions posed by the computer. I was one of those students who spend much of their class time surfing the Web or intermittently playing computer games, so I tried to take notes by hand for a semester. It caused me to pay attention a little better, but I soon found others ways to distract myself and began to lose whatever advantage I had gained by shunning the PC. Eventually I returned to using the computer and just made a conscious effort to resist the distractions, though I often failed. As a general rule I think you are better off using a computer in class to take notes. At least give it a try.

Law students frequently use different software to take notes. My first year, I took notes in Microsoft Word. Halfway through law school I noticed many other students were using Microsoft One Note, so I switched. I never really appreciated much difference, but I continued using One Note for no particular reason. The content of the notes, rather than how they were saved, mattered most to me. Newer software options may offer some meaningful choices. Aspen's Study Desk software package has a way to take notes that is designed to make it easier to integrate them into a later outline. I do not have personal experience using it, and I am not sure how much of an advantage it offers. I would encourage you to be open-minded on the software you use to make notes, but I generally suggest using software you are comfortable with. The real focus here is on learning and retaining the material, and spending too much time messing around with new software you are unfamiliar with can undermine your learning.

Recording Classes

Should you record class lectures? Even if your professor allows you to record classes, your daily 1L classes are not generally worth recording. My first-year contracts professor recorded all of his classes and made the MP3s available to students, and other professors permitted students to record the lectures on their laptops. Two weeks before the exam I decided to listen to the MP3s from class while cleaning. I had been worried about the sound quality. The sound was fine, but the MP3s were useless. Most of the talking in law school classes in which the Socratic method is used is done by students. It takes an hour to get a few sentences of quality material out of the mouths of students. The case method means that much of what is discussed in class are the particular facts of the case, not the law or application of law that you must know for exams. Law school class recordings will include 50 minutes of your peers' "ummms" and "uhhhhhs" as they give inadequate answers to the professor's questions and five to ten minutes of useful material. There are several reasons that commercial audio lectures cover in six hours what a law school class takes a semester to cover; one is the dead time, filler, and wrong answers from students. Some professors actually lecture, and these may be worth recording if they give you permission. Final reviews prior to exams may be worth recording. But as a general rule, recording your daily classes is not worth the trouble and listening to the recordings is not the best use of your time.

Being Active Without Being Hated as a Gunner

Class participation might give you a grade boost, but the wrong kind of participation can undermine your grade and your relationship with your professor. Being seen as a "gunner" can also hurt your relationships with your peers. There is a fine line to walk here, and perhaps the truest gunner thing to do is to be a gunner without being hated or perceived as one.

Participating in Class Without Being Hated by Your Peers

Some bright students are hesitant to volunteer in class because they do not want to be labeled a *gunner*, an obviously overambitious student. Law school parody videos mock gunners, and there is a real hatred toward them. This cannot be explained exclusively by jealousy. Some gunners do very well in life, but some are just annoying. I personally hated the people I considered to be *false* gunners. False gunners are individuals who don't know what they are talking about and are not actually all that bright, but who love to talk and hear the sound of their own voice. If you are focused or nervous enough to read this book, that is probably not you. If you do know your material but do not want to come off as a know-it-all, then be respectful to your peers and considerate of their feelings.

The easiest way to do this is to not talk just to hear the sound of your own voice. Just because you know the answer does not mean you need to let people know. Do not bash or mock classmates behind their backs for getting an answer wrong or sounding stupid. Even if your statements do not get back to them, you will develop a bad reputation. When a classmate has been called on and is getting the answer wrong, handle it delicately. If the professor calls on you to sort out the mess the other person made, consider both your word choice and tone. Talking with too much confidence can make your peers feel like they had stupid answers. It might be worth it to actually add a little bit of uncertainty to your voice when called on to correct or disagree with a peer. Too much false uncertainty will be seen right through, but if you are confident enough while seeming unconfident sometimes, you can avoid being hated. And if you volunteer to jump in when a classmate is dying and getting it wrong, try to set yourself up to defend and bail out your peer rather than undermine him or her. Treat your classmate as mostly right or needing help articulating the point, rather than as a moron. Your professors will still know that you are the one with the right answer.

How to Impress or Get to Know Your Law Professor Without Being Seen as a Brownnoser

Getting to know your law professor allows you to impress him or her. This may seem obvious, but very few students take the time to get to know their professors. Impressing your law professor helps you out in numerous ways, including receiving a possible discretionary participation boost in your final grade, earning a letter of recommendation from that professor for future jobs, landing a research assistant job with that professor, and creating a good working relationship, which makes it easier for you to get help with problem areas within that class or to get help on other projects and papers outside that class. Understanding your professor can help you get inside his or her head, giving you a better sense of what kind of material will be on the exam and what kind of answers he or she likes, but being seen as a brownnoser undermines all of this.

Law students hate gunners, and professors do not necessarily like them either. Nobody really likes a brownnoser. It is best to impress your professor without coming across as someone who is trying overly hard to impress or suck up to the professor. Doing well in class requires more than just showing up on time and staying until the class ends. As a starting point, you should look good in class by doing your reading and volunteering answers when no one else will, or when no one else is right, but not every single time. Make sure you always know what you are saying in class or, at the very least, that your questions are thoughtful. In other words, think before you raise your hand. It is not necessary to always agree with your professor; respectfully disagreeing with and challenging your professor can make your professor respect you and provide a helpful intellectual exercise for your class. But do not let your disagreement clog or overwhelm classroom discussion. Remember that you can ask questions after class, chat with your professor in the hall, or follow up on class discussions over e-mail. You can also follow up to develop your personal interests—for instance, if you are interested in discussing some area in more depth than your class has time for or if you want to ask your professor to recommend reading on a particular topic. Do not pester your professors, though. If trying to get to know them is not working, then leave them alone. Putting in at least some effort means that they probably know your name for a good reason, and this is better than nothing.

Pay attention to what your professors are doing outside of the classroom. At the very least, read their CVs or bios on the law school's Web site. If a professor is participating in a debate or as a lunchtime speaker at your school, attend the event and get noticed. If you are pressed for time, bring one of your books with you and try to study discreetly at the back of the room. And take advantage of other opportunities that are offered. Some schools have programs where professors go out to lunch with their students. My 1L property professor tried to get a small group of students together to discuss jurisprudence over pizza in the evening. Professors are often interesting and always smart, so it is worth getting to know them. You can also get to know them through their writing.

Some professors write blogs, and if yours do, you should read them. Most professors do a great deal of scholarly writing, often about the topics they teach in class. By looking at their publication list, you can quickly get a sense of their research agenda. If your torts professor writes almost exclusively about libel and slander, this might be helpful to know when prioritizing what to study for the exam. If you have the time, try to read some of your professors' writings, at least those that relate to the subject of your class. If your law school has a decent faculty Web site, your professor's page will provide you with citations for his or her scholarship and possibly links to public versions on the Social Science Research Network (SSRN). If you cannot find a list, a LexisNexis or Westlaw search of law reviews and journal articles with your professor's name in the author field should provide what you need. A cursory examination of the titles and abstracts (summaries) will tell you a lot about your professor, the topics he or she cares about, and his or her approach to them. If the articles are highly relevant to your class, it might be worth reading or at least skimming them all.

I did this for my election law class. The professor wrote about exactly what she was teaching in class and had a large but manageable body of scholarly work. I printed all of her election law articles and started reading them. I was very impressed with her abilities as a writer and realized I could learn more than election law from these articles. I did not, however, have time to read every word of them. Instead, I focused on three things. I examined the conclusions to try to understand my professor's ideological orientation and ultimate resolution of the issues. I also scanned the articles for any discussion or treatment of cases, which I circled at the time and later read. Seeing how my professor described a case in one sentence or finding out what she thought the outcome really meant helped me in class and with the exam. Finally, I tried to identify some of the key phrases—buzzwords, if you will—that my professor used to describe the major concepts in our course so that I could try to use a similar word structure in framing my answers. The process worked out well for me and also benefited my study partner, with whom I shared a condensed version of what I learned.

Knowing your professor can help you pick out the right things when reading cases for class and better articulate answers on exams. Once you establish some understanding of your professor and a healthy working relationship with him or her, you will naturally find more things to connect on. If you know your criminal procedure professor's research interest involves the wrongly accused and problems in plea bargaining and you read a newspaper article about a mentally ill person falsely confessing to a crime, you will automatically think to share it with the professor and possibly talk about it later. After you have put the time in to establish this relationship, try to keep in touch later as you take other classes and move into the work force. Your professor's insight, or recommendation, could still be helpful in the future.

Key Points

- Class participation affects your grade, but usually only by a discretionary boost (one-third of a grade; A– to A). So be prepared for class, but don't spend too much time worrying about your participation.
- A good case brief should cover the essential facts of the case, the lower court holding, the procedural posture (how this case came to the appellate court), the issue for the court to decide, the rule of law produced by the court in this case, and the result (who won the case).
- The three-step process of case briefing:
  - Step 1: Brief the case completely to get the hang of the information you should know.
  - Step 2: Read each case twice, once to get the overall idea and once to take notes and comprehend. "Book brief" by writing notes on the margins of the brief in a shorthand you can easily understand and refer to in class.
  - Step 3: Only write, and rely on for class discussion, margin notes. Be sure to include a very succinct summary at the top of the brief to remind yourself what the case is about.
- Be sure to note when you fail to recognize what the correct answer is, so that you can retrain your instincts.
- Remember to be mindful of your professor's views and interests when writing out notes and when briefing cases.
- Figure out the key facts and necessary info when taking notes in class, and filter out student gibberish that occurs in the course of Socratic dialogue.
- Learn what method of note-taking (on a computer or by hand, for instance, or recording or not recording classes) works for you and stick to it. Avoid complicated systems and avoid spending more time on learning the method than on taking notes.

- To be a gunner without being hated, be mindful of your tone and manner in and out of the classroom, especially when among your peers. Avoid mocking other students for wrong answers, and be respectful when called on by a professor to correct another student's incorrect response.
- To get to know your professor without becoming a brownnoser, read about your professor's interests on the school's Web site and look up their writings on the Internet to get an idea of how they approach the law and what their interests are. Do not push talking to them or developing the relationship if they seem uninterested, but do try, as the networking opportunities are beneficial.

Chapter 4

PREPARING FOR EXAMS AND LEARNING THE LAW

The Big Picture Approach to Classes, and How to Study for the Final Exam Before Class Has Even Begun

GRASPING HOW IMPORTANT EXAMS ARE IS THE FIRST STEP to seeing the big picture. The exam is all that matters. Class is a means to an end. Your grade is based on how well you do on the exam, not how well you do in class, with a few exceptions. Law school classes are full of discussions about facts of cases and dissents. A chunk of time is wasted with wrong answers and silly arguments. There is some connection between the class and the final exam, but it is not a perfect correlation.

Most people spend all of their study time preparing for class. They languish over trying to understand the facts of a case—facts they are not tested on. Many students do not put any effort into studying for the one thing that is graded until they finish the last day of class. Now, if you are not yet in law school, this might surprise you. You might assume there is something wrong with these students or they just do not get it. But try reading an 1820s civil procedure case and preparing to talk about it the next day and see how much free time you end up with. The daily grind of the 1L year is just plain hard. Because it's so hard, many students spend all of their time looking at only what is right in front of them. This is generally the stack of casebooks and the reading list for the next day, with some legal writing homework included. On the final exam, though, you are tested on the big picture. You are required to apply all the torts you learned and all the defenses at once, not just an individual tort at a time. This is why you need to be able to see the big picture—the entire subject at once.

Someone gave me the suggestion of reading an outline of the class all the way before a semester started, or at least very early in the semester. The suggestion was to read it, not study it, just read through it. This could be a commercial supplement, a full-on treatise, or a senior student's old outline. Reading an outline at the start of the semester will not teach you the law. It is possible you may learn snippets, but most of material will not make sense on a quick read-through. The point of this plunge through an outline is to get a sense of what is coming. If you know the kind of material you will see in a class, you can better understand what a particular case or class topic means and where it fits with the rest of the semester and subject.

During my first semester, I found a particular part of contracts very difficult at first. I was struggling to understand the UCC 2-207 "Battle of the Forms" cases. These are commercial contract cases with relatively complicated procedures and facts, not to mention the legal issues involved. It just was not clicking with me. Even though I could read and somewhat comprehend the individual cases, I felt lost. They were clearly about contracts, and there was a law, but I didn't know what I was supposed to get out of them at all. I had followed my friend's advice and read the *CrunchTime* capsule summaries (commercial outlines) for my other classes, but I just had not found the time to read them for contracts. Finally, I forced myself to find the time.

Reading the outline sections dealing with the Battle of Forms was helpful, but seeing where these sections were placed within the overall outline was even more helpful to me. The legal issue involved was offer and acceptance as a part of the formation process. This subtopic fit into the broader theme of whether a contract was formed and, if so, what are the legally binding terms of the contract. For me, this was a huge breakthrough. Now I knew what I was supposed to learn from this unit and the individual cases within it. It all started to click with me.

I think all law students can benefit from being able to see the big picture and looking beyond the shortsighted daily struggle to simply survive the grind. It is helpful to skim through an outline again later in the semester to keep the big picture in mind. Looking through your professor's syllabus or even the table of the contents of the casebook can also be helpful if you are doing it for the specific purpose of seeing where things fit and why they are in that particular order.

Reading an outline before the semester begins helps you to see the big picture of the course but also the big picture of what matters in the class: learning the law and being able to apply it on the exam. It is important to get yourself focused on the final exam from the get-go. With this focus, you can get more out of class because you realize that each class can help you on the final exam. Outside of class, you need to find time over the course of the semester to focus on learning the law. Whether it is reading a commercial supplement, listening to an audio CD, or even reviewing the black-letter law in your notes, you need to set aside some time for learning law other than just keeping up with the daily grind. The same is true after the first year.

At some point, law school gets easier. It might be after your first year, or even after the first semester if you are fortunate. The daily grind is not as crazy once reading cases comes easier. Many people simply stop working as hard. Instead, you should use this newfound time to work smarter. Instead of watching more TV, start your final exam prep earlier. Seeing the big picture in law school itself means knowing that the final exam is the key. If you can keep that in mind over the course of the semester, you can do quite well.

Key Points

- Class is a means to an end because your grade is usually based on how well you do on the exam, not how well you do in class.
- Exams will test on the big picture, applying all the law you learned.
- Reading an outline at the start of the semester will not give you mastery of the subject, but it will give you a better sense of what is coming, allowing you to see, as you go along in class, where information fits in the scope of the course.

Outlining

Given how much first-years talk about—and stress about—their outlines, you would think they are very hard things to make. An outline is not a hard thing to make; it just takes time. Work on it, but do not stress about it. And do not consider it sacred. "Go to class, take notes, and prepare an outline" is the typical, standard law school advice. It works for most people, but like everything in this book, you have to evaluate how you think it will work for you, and after you try it, you have to evaluate whether it worked. Outlining is a great device for some students. One student I knew spent a great deal of time preparing outlines and credited her outlining strategy for her law school success. She found practice questions useless. I, on the other hand, never made a really decent law school outline (although I paid attention to what others did to make good outlines). I credit practice questions for all of my success. If you are going to make an outline, you should make a good one.

How to Outline

An outline should be a concise presentation of legal material covered in your class. This means it should present the *law* learned in class, not the *facts*. Primarily, this means the black-letter law—the legal rule and conclusion from a case—and not the case itself. Case names usually do not matter unless the case is huge. In some classes, like Constitutional Law, almost every case is huge. Also, some professors really like you to know case names, which means they should be in your outline. And even when case names do matter, usually only the most important facts of the case matter—a sentence's worth. Much of your discussion in class may center on the facts of a case, but your exam will test you on the law. You need to know enough of the facts to be able to recognize a case from the fact pattern presented on the exam, but always remember that you are being tested on the law. Generally, you can create your outline by using your class notes and the notes or briefing you put together from the casebook. It can be helpful to have a commercial outline or treatise handy to check the outline you create against and to look up topics that you found confusing. If you think your notes have accurately captured what the professor said but they seem to contradict the treatise, err on the side of trusting your professor—but ask him or her about it to make sure you have it right. Your class and case notes will probably be in the same order in which the subjects were covered in class. This is a good way to organize your outline. Your professor chose to structure and order the class in a particular way, and there presumably is a very good reason for doing so. If your outline lines up with this structure, hopefully it will help your thinking line up with your professor's. When to outline also depends on why you are outlining. Those who create the best, nicest outlines do it over the course of the semester. They try to keep their outlines as up-to-date as they can. In a perfect world, they would set aside time each weekend to update their outline with what was covered the previous week. Those who outline exclusively as an exam aid wait to the end of the semester. Procrastinators wait to the end or fail to do it all. If outlining sounds like something that would help you, it is probably best to do it over the course of the semester to reduce the burden at the end. Style is a matter of personal choice. Many students put their outlines in a typical . . . well, outline form using the headings and options available in their software. For example:

I. Intentional Torts
    a. Battery
       i. Elements:
          1. An act by the defendant
          2. Intent to cause harmful or offensive contact
          3. Harmful or offensive contact results

This is fine, and it works for many people. It also produces a lot of white space, which means more pages to flip through when studying, more paper to carry around, and more pages to look through when trying to find something. One of the best sets of outlines I've ever seen maximized the amount of text on a page by combining small margins, tight writing, and a simple paragraph form rather than the usual outline style (as described above). The first page of the second semester tort's outline is set out in Figure 1.

In addition to capturing the content well, I think this outline does a great job of using bold text to capture and draw your attention to the things that you should pay attention to. Also note the use of shorthand, such as "AoR" after "Assumption of the Risk" appears, "P" for plaintiff, and "D" for defendant. If you can use shorthand that you will immediately recognize, it can make your outline much more concise. You should not start with a specific goal for how long your outline should be. It should be as long as it needs to be to capture and convey the law covered in your class. A monstrously long outline is not very useful. But rather than setting an artificial limit on length, start by including everything that seems relevant and then begin to cut and tweak the language. Some of the best outliners start with a pretty long outline going into the exam period and end with a relatively short final product. The outline excerpted in Figure 1 is a total of 20.5 pages long with 0.25-inch margins. But even if there is room to tweak or cut it more, at some point you have to start studying and stop fiddling with it.

What to Do with the Outline

What should you do with the outline? Read it. Then read the sections you didn't understand well again, and again, until you at least have the material in your memory. Then work on applying law to facts through practice questions, returning to

Figure 1. Torts II Course Outline

Comparative Negligence

Comparative Negligence allows recovery proportional to each party's **relative degree of fault**. Recovery is not barred for a plaintiff's negligence, but only reduced based on his contribution to the injury (determined by the jury). **Two types: Pure** or strict, and **modified. Pure form** = P's damages reduced in direct proportion to the percentage negligence attributed to him (i.e. a ninety percent negligent plaintiff can still get 10 percent damages). The **modified** form says you can recover as in pure jurisdictions, but you can only do so if **P's negligence either does not exceed fifty percent, or is less than 49%. "Less than" (less than fifty percent):** Some jurisdictions apply the rule that the plaintiff's negligence must be **less than** the defendant's. If the plaintiff was **fifty percent or more** negligent, he cannot recover; recovery is allowed if the plaintiff contributed up to 49 percent. **"Not greater than" (fifty percent or less):** Other jurisdictions state that if the plaintiff's negligence is **"not greater than"** the defendant's, he may recover. Thus, the plaintiff's and the defendant's negligence may be **equal** and the plaintiff may still recover. For multiple Ds, P can recover so long as P's fault is less than the combined fault of the Ds. **Unit rule** or individual rule—do you compare P's fault to each D, or to the Ds as a unit? Majority is modified fifty percent, minorities are pure and modified 49 percent. Things like last clear chance doctrine and assumption of risk are no longer needed—they are taken into consideration when apportioning liability.

Assumption of Risk

Express Assumption of Risk: Really, this is about **contracts**. An **exculpatory clause** is sufficient to insulate the party from his or her own negligence so long as its language clearly and specifically indicates the **intent to release the defendant from liability for personal injury caused by the defendant's negligence. Exceptions:** when harm is **intentional or conduct is reckless, wanton, or gross;** when **bargaining power** is **unequal** such that contract becomes a **contract** of **adhesion;** and when transaction involves the public interest. For a contract to be one of adhesion, the service offered must be a necessity. For public policy, there are several factors, but you must look to the **totality of the circumstances.** Express AoR is a complete defense.

Implied Assumption of Risk: The fundamental difference between an implied assumption of risk and contributory negligence is the **element of willingness.**

For AoR, you know about the risk, and willingly undertake it. For contributory negligence, you should have known about the risk had you exercised due care. AoR is **subjective**—did this person assume the risk? Contributory negligence is objective—the reasonable prudent person standard.

There are two types of implied AoR—**primary** and **secondary**. Under secondary, there are two types—**pure** or strict, and **qualified**. The real question is whether this is still viable under a comparative negligence doctrine. Implied primary AoR is another way of saying D was not negligent, either because there is no duty or no breach of duty, and it is subsumed in the principle of negligence itself. Secondary implied AoR is an affirmative defense to an established breach of duty. **Strict or pure** is when P acted reasonably (rushing into a burning house to save a child). **Qualifed** is when P acts unreasonably (rushing into a burning house to save a fedora). All are rejected under the doctrine of negligence except for pure or strict, since it is important to recognize reasonableness.

Statute of Limitations

Traditional rule is that the cause of action accrues at the date of the injury. **Discovery rule**—cause of action accrues when P discovers or should have discovered the injury. Only in medical malpractice cases. **Continuing torts** are viewed as the cause of action accruing at the completion of the tort (i.e. battered wife). **Statutes of repose**: limits the time in which a cause of action can arise. This is not about when you can sue, but when there can be a cause of action at all.

Immunities

Different from privileges. Relate to status, not to circumstances. Immunity does not deny tort, but simply says absolution from liability is granted.

Interspousal Immunity—Majority of courts reject interspousal immunity, which prevented one spouse from suing another for negligence actions. A minority recognizes limited exceptions, such as for intentional torts.

Parent-child—Trend is to abrogate the immunity and permit recovery for child-parent suits, whereas a minority allows the immunity but also allows exceptions.

consult (or modify) your outline whenever you struggle with a question or do not understand something. Read it again during the exam study period, and read it all the way through on the eve of the exam. Your outline is a great resource to help you practice applying law to facts as you work through an issue. It can also help you spot issues in a practice fact pattern by seeing which topics on the outline are contained in the fact pattern.

Why to Outline and Alternatives to Making Your Own Outline

Now that you have taken all these notes in class, you probably feel the need to do something with them. Outlining gives you a focused tool to help you prepare for the exam. It is something to consult when answering practice questions. It is also a great study aid on its own as something to review during the exam period. As you try to cram more and more into your head during finals, you are going to end up forgetting things and becoming confused about things you once knew. Your own outline, which reflects your own knowledge back when it was fresh in your head, can be very helpful in jogging your memory. Most students claim to get the real benefit out of *making* the outline. Focusing their thoughts on the outline and the process of making the outline over the course of the semester, or at the end of the semester, is a tremendous mental exercise and a learning experience. If this is why you outline, and it really works for you, then keep doing it in future semesters. But just because it works, does not mean it works best for you. Spending dozens of hours preparing an outline forces you to learn material. But spending dozens of hours on almost any subject probably would force you to learn a lot of material. The question is whether this is the most efficient way for you to learn.

During my first semester in law school, I tried to keep up with my outlines. They were not all that good, but I was at least making a real effort. At some point a friend sent me an outline prepared by a student who was a year ahead of me and had been in my section with the same professors and the same casebooks. He was a legend. Not only had he pulled a 4.0, but his outlines were amazing and widely circulated. When I looked at his outlines, an excerpt from which is included in Figure 1, I realized they were so much better than anything I could produce and so perfect for what I needed, I decided to give up making my own. I spent my time studying his outlines and doing practice questions. That worked best for me—practice questions and outlines prepared by someone else—and I stuck with that routine in the future, although nobody gave me perfect outlines in the future and I often relied on commercial outlines. Commercial supplements can include outlines, and they can even be keyed to your casebook, but they are not keyed to your professor and your class. If you want an outline keyed to your professor without doing the work, you are going to need to get one made by a fellow student. And it is unlikely that someone will generously give you the perfect outline. Some students do swap outlines with each other. In the movie *The Paper Chase*, the members of a study group divided classes among themselves, with each student taking responsibility for a class. This means putting a lot of faith in your fellow students. I liked taking classes with my friend Clayton because he made very solid outlines and was willing to share them with me. Unfortunately, I could not take every class with him. When I was a law student at the University of Michigan, student groups maintained outline banks for their members. Many were outdated and only marginally useful—I only used them with pass/fail classes. You can ask around at your school. Some Web sites maintain free outline banks: see, for instance, *http://www.legalnut.com/outlines/*. It may also be worth Googling to see what new resources are out there.

Suggesting that a student could avoid making an outline, study something else, and still do well is probably considered heresy to most people who work at a law school. Back in law school, I certainly thought of myself as a heretic in this regard. I felt that new options made the old rules less important. Only recently have I realized that I was not as radical as I thought. While I never made a full twenty- or sixty-page outline, I did make a small outline for every class. Sometimes it was two handwritten pages created while studying; sometimes it was a two- to three-page typed document. I did not outline the entire class; I outlined only the topics that were particularly difficult for me or that I thought would be most helpful if I had an open-book exam. I did these little outlines at the very end of the semester, possibly the day before the exam, when I knew exactly what material I might struggle with. That was the only outlining I needed to do to excel in law school.

Key Points

- Outlines should concisely present the law learned in class, not lots of facts, but include case names if your professor would like you to know them.
- If you outline, do it over the course of the semester to reduce the burden of outlining the whole thing at the end of the course when prepping for exams.

■ Outlining can provide mental exercise and a learning experience that can aid in mastering the material.

■ If outlining does not work for you or is too inefficient, there is no shame in forgoing outline creation and using a method that works better for you.

■ Good commercial outlines can provide some of the benefits of outlining, as can school banks of outlines or good peer outlines. But because they may be unreliable and always lack information specific to your professor, take them with a grain of salt.

The Question and Answer Method

I am a huge believer in using a question-and-answer approach both to learn the law and to study for law school exams, for the reasons set out in this chapter. Law school exams test your ability to apply the law to facts. You are not required to simply regurgitate the rule against perpetuities; you need to be able to figure out whether any given interest violates or does not violate the rule. In my view, the best way to learn how to apply law to facts is to practice applying law to facts.

But like any law school study tactic, the question-and-answer method works better for some than others. I know a student who was very successful in law school and completely rejected using practice questions to study. Although I personally suspect she would have done even better if her studying routine had included practice questions, she did quite well by simply memorizing the law through drilling herself on her outline. You should include practice questions in your studying routine until and unless you find that other methods work better for you. And even if you are confident that outline memorization will be the best way for you to learn, you should still include at least some practice questions in preparing for the exam.

Using Practice Questions to Prepare for the Final Exam
Why You Need Practice Questions

Law school exams usually test your analysis more than your memory. Knowing the elements of a tort is essential for a torts exam and is, quite frankly, expected; knowing how to apply those elements and analyze a fact pattern is required for a good answer. The tricky questions require you to spot small details, understand the significance of those details, notice what details are not contained in the question, and provide a nuanced answer. They do not require you to simply memorize and regurgitate a detailed list. Your professor is likely going to test your ability to spot issues in fact patterns, so you should prepare by practicing with that type of question.

When my wife, Karen, was studying anatomy as an undergraduate, she had both an anatomy class and an anatomy lab. The anatomy class required and tested on rote memorization—Karen had to memorize all sorts of body parts and their purpose, action, location, connection, and innervation (something about the nerves). Karen learned this material by drilling with flash cards (she purchased some commercial supplements but also made her own to be sure they provided the exact details she needed for class). Once she knew the material, she knew it. At the same time, she was taking an anatomy class that required her to identify organs inside an actual dead body in the lab. It is much more difficult to spot an organ inside a cut-open cadaver than it is to memorize where the organ is supposed to be or what it does. Generally, science students are not permitted to touch the organs, and the tissues all look the same—the differences are very subtle. The way to prepare for the anatomy lab was to attend open lab hours and practice spotting the same organs in the same cadavers that would be used for the exam—and it was still difficult. Aside from the obvious differences, issue-spotting in law school is more like organ spotting in a cadaver. Just as Karen had to adjust her studying strategies to reflect the nature of the test, you need to adjust your studying methods to reflect what law school exams test.

Once again I'll insert the caveat that goes with every section in this book: Study for what your professor is testing you on. If you have a civil procedure professor who tells you that she will be testing on specific numbers of the rules of civil procedure or will have an exam with fill-in-the-blank or multiple-choice questions involving how many depositions a party is normally allowed to take, your studying strategy should involved rote memorization and typical undergraduate memorization methods like simple flash cards. But if your professor is going to test you with a typical issue-spotting question (discussed in Chapter 5), you need to prepare and practice with those type of questions in mind by creating at least a detailed outline that spots and analyzes the issues involved. Getting good practice questions is one of the most important steps.

Where to Get Practice Questions

The absolute best practice questions for preparing for a professor's exam are the questions on that professor's prior exams. Previous exams are valuable not only for the practice possibilities but also for the insight you can gain into your professor and his or her style. Some professors provide students with copies of select prior exams during the course of the semester.

Some schools have organized ways of preserving prior exams—paper copies in the library or some kind of online system. Look into this. If you have a visiting professor who used to teach at another school, try to get her past exams from that school—if you do not have any friends there, start by calling the school's library. Ideally, but less commonly, you will get model answers from the professors. If you do not have a model answer, you may find it helpful to either try answering it in a group or develop an answer independently and then compare notes with friends.

Your professors may not make any prior exams available, and if they do provide some, they might not be enough to thoroughly prepare you. In this case, you can turn to commercial supplements for practice essay questions and model answers. Practicing with commercial questions and answers is not as productive as using an exam prepared by your professor, but it is better than nothing and still provides an opportunity to practice applying law to facts.

Answering Questions as a Group

When your professor gives you a practice question without a model answer, you can get together with a group of fellow students to try to come up with a collective answer. This method essentially has the pluses and minuses of a Wikipedia entry. Keep that in mind.

Some people love answering practice exam questions in groups. You will see them in study rooms looking very serious and writing on whiteboards. I am skeptical of how much studying such groups actually accomplish, but do not let my skepticism keep you from joining one. I did join some group answer discussions, but I mostly did this to be social. I think it depends on your personality and the personalities in the rest of the group. What worked best for me was to answer questions with my buddy Clayton. He was very nose-to-the-grindstone and kept me from chatting or getting off-topic. He was quite smart and had good answers, sometimes with different reasons than mine. Overall, how you check your answers against others' probably falls into the category of things to continue to fine-tune over the course of your law school career.

Using Practice Questions to Learn Throughout the Semester

Using questions just before the exam is common; using questions earlier in the semester is far less common. I am a big fan of using practice questions to study during the semester for three reasons.

1. They test retention. Some commercial supplements include a handful of practice questions at the end of each chapter to make sure you got the material. So much is going into your head during law school that I think it can be helpful to know if it sticks.
2. They identify strengths and weaknesses early. Some things only seem hard when you test on them, other things sound hard but test easier. For example, I, like most others, find the rule against perpetuities hard to understand and somewhat terrifying to read: "Any interest must vest, if at all, not later than 21 years after a life in being at the creation of the interest." But I found that questions on the rule were surprisingly easy for me to answer. Other topics, like probable cause, made perfect sense to me but were shockingly hard to answer when given fact patterns. Practice questions can help you know yourself.
3. They can work with your institution and flag problems. A lot of things in law are instinctive. You have probably lived in the United States for all or most of your life. You have probably watched U.S. television and gotten a college degree in the United States. Much of our law is reflected in our culture, and much of our law reflects our values. Consider self-defense, for example. Without needing to read about the law of self-defense, you can probably guess the right answer to a simple fact pattern involving a self-defense issue. At the same time, you might guess wrong on the law of citizen's arrest. For whatever reason, this legal issue is never really presented in the media. Perhaps that is because Batman or other vigilantes never stick around to face personal tort or criminal liability. Knowing which subjects fit your intuition and which ones do not can be very helpful in focusing your studying.

I loved using Aspen's "Law in a Flash" cards for just this purpose. I completed the cards early in the semester and pulled out the ones I got wrong to use repeatedly, figuring that if there was something off on my instincts on that topic, it would need extra work. There are other supplements that can be used, as set out later in this chapter. There are whole books of practice questions, and some books include practice questions at the end of each chapter.

I always found practice questions helpful to study. I saw my friend Jeff using them before I started law school and made a point to use them from the very beginning. Essentially, I used products marketed as final exam aids to learn for class. They made me think about legal issues early, and that worked for me. Many, perhaps most, successful students do not employ practice questions until the end of the semester, and some do not emphasize them at all.

I had confidence that I would learn the material by the end of the semester, so I was okay with getting a lot of questions wrong at first. Other folks could have the opposite reaction. Early wrong answers might derail confidence and discourage you. Try doing some practice questions early on to see if they work for you. If they do, use them throughout the semester. If not, just wait until exam time and reevaluate the tactic each semester.

Studying Differently for Different Subjects

A friend once asked me whether he should use different study tactics for different subjects. I suggested that it is more important to change your study tactics for different professors and their classes than for the subject matter of the class, but there may be some common differences in subject matter that could guide your studying. The difference between upper-level electives like Federal Antitrust and Law and Shakespeare is obvious.

Torts and criminal law exams, for example, often ask you to know elements. In torts, the elements and defenses get you the points on the exam. Civil procedure requires you to learn the rules and possibly the numbers for those rules, depending on your professor. With civil procedure, it may be helpful to actually draw things out on scratch paper when you're dealing with issues like joining third parties and counter-claims and cross-claims. Property, on the other hand, may require prioritization.

Property often feels like a hodgepodge of discrete and unrelated topics—*inter vivos* gifts and easements by their natures seem less related to each other than assault and battery. With property, keying in on the subtopics and areas that matter most to your professor is even more important. But be careful not to take this too far. I was convinced that my property professor would not test on lost, found, and buried property because of the speed with which we moved through that material and my perceptions of what the professor wanted us to focus on. My property exam tested on a bunch of different subjects, including a party digging up a watch (or something like that). I was forced to strain to remember material from classes months earlier and just guess. I was wrong about whether buried treasure would be on the exam, but I was mostly right about what else was on the exam and still pulled an A. With property, you need to have enough knowledge to deal with any topic covered in class, but the material is so diverse that you do need to prioritize studying.

Key Points

- Practice answering questions that involve fact pattern issue-spotting, not just regurgitating the rules and laws.
- Access practice questions from prior exams if possible. Some schools have ways of organizing these at a library or in an online system.
- Consider whether group studying is a productive tool for you; use it if it is, avoid it if it is not.
- Practice questions test retention, help identify strengths and weaknesses to focus on, and help you train your instincts to be correct.
- Aspen's "Law in a Flash" cards can be very helpful.

Using Study Aids and Commercial Supplements

It shocks me how some law students are willing to spend $30,000 on tuition but will not spend $30 for a study aid to get better grades in law school. Law school grades influence what jobs you land, and thus what salary you earn after graduation. They might gain you (or lose you) scholarships at your law school and from outside organizations. Why a student who would spend $10,000–$50,000 per year would balk at spending $200 on study aids a semester is beyond my understanding. Perhaps it is because somebody else is paying for the tuition, or tuition is paid directly by student loans while study aid money comes out of a student's wallet. But cheaping out on study aids is irrational.

Commercial study aids, if used properly, will improve your grades. Better grades, if marketed properly, will set you up for scholarships and jobs. In my opinion, the return on investment with study aids is probably greater than the return on investment with law school. In this section, I cover the types of commercial supplements available, describe some of the best practices in using them, and offer some advice on how to pick the right strategy for you.

The Study Aids

I am defining study aids broadly to include materials available to help you understand the law and prepare for exams other than your textbook or the outlines you make yourself or get from classmates. I am not referring to the "supplement" that may come with your textbook itself (e.g., a supplement containing the Federal Rules of Civil Procedure that comes with your Civ Pro book). I am not including canned case briefs to help you prepare for class because those are covered in Chapter 3.

Your campus or law school bookstore might sell a few supplements, and your library might have some too, but do not limit yourself to the selection in your neighborhood—if you think one of these items will help you excel in class, find it online and buy it. Even though I bought my supplements online, for the first two years of law school I mostly bought products that would have been available locally because I was familiar with them. During my third year, I took a class (Federal Antitrust) where commercial supplements were harder to find than a class where the format of the exam (tricky multiple-choice questions) forced me to find as many practice multiple-choice questions for the topic as possible.

The law school market for commercial supplements is significant, and lots of publishers provide a bewildering supply of choices. Publishers tend to focus on the most popular classes, which means that certain supplements are not available for certain subjects (you can get pre-made flashcards for Torts but not for Antitrust). To help you wade through your options, I have broken them down into six categories.

Treatises and hornbooks.

These books tend to be physically large and are written in actual prose. Popular examples include Erwin Chemerinsky books on constitutional law and federal jurisdiction in the *Introduction to Law* series. These books tend to actually explain the topics and the law, which is a big improvement over casebooks. Professors also like these books and may view them as the only "acceptable" commercial study aid.

When moving away from academic acceptability and toward practicality, you find *Nutshells*. The *Nutshell* series consists of physically small treatises. These little books give you an overview of the subject that you can actually read all the way through without great difficulty and can take with you easily. *Nutshells* are usually written in easy-to-understand language, to the extent it is possible to use understandable language with legal topics. *Examples and Explanations* provides explanatory text in a normal book style, but follows that up with a series of questions. For some students, these questions can be a great way to ensure that they understand the material.

Outline + testing aids.

Another category of commercial supplements include an outline (called *commercial outlines* to distinguish them from student-made products) along with testing aids. Commercial outlines offer a significant advantage over casebooks (and to some extent, treatises) in that the bright-line rules are quite literally underlined with a bright line and the black-letter law is written out in bolded, black letters to stand out. The disadvantage, of course, in using a commercial product is that it is not keyed to your professor. It is an outline of tort law, not tort law according to Professor Miller. But if you approach them with this understanding, these products can be very helpful. It is standard for commercial outlines to include a variety of testing aids in the back of the book (and sometimes throughout it).

More substantial (larger) products include the *Emanuel Law Outlines* series, which features a short capsule summary, detailed outline with short-answer questions and exam tips at the end of each chapter, essay exam questions and answers, and a glossary. *Gilbert's* is Thomson West's version of *Emanuel* and also includes a summary, a detailed outline, and some practice questions. The *Sum & Substance Quick Review* is another Thomson West product with more content that offers the same formula. All of these larger commercial outlines are helpful in the same ways; picking among them is basically a matter of taste.

The market also includes smaller products. *CrunchTime* is essentially a stripped-down version of the *Emanuel* outline. It features flow charts, a capsule summary (about 100 pages long), exam tips, and a variety of practice questions (multiple choice, short answer, and essay). Much of the content is borrowed from *Emanuel*, so there's usually no reason to get both. Kaplan PMBR's *Finals* series is a competitor for *CrunchTime*, but not as good or as well known, in my opinion. LexisNexis's *Questions & Answers* series fits in this same niche.

Straight testing aids.

Commercial outlines include some practice questions, but you can also find products with only practice questions and answers. The *Siegel's* series by Aspen includes practice essay and practice multiple-choice questions. Thomson West offers a similar series called *Exam Pro*, although the copy I used for a class only included multiple choice questions while the *Siegel's* included both multiple-choice and essay questions, as did my professor's exam. If you are facing a multiple-choice only exam, *Siegel's* might be more useful. Both of these products offer substantially more practice questions than do the commercial outlines, which means if you are looking to do a lot of practice questions (such as when you are preparing for a multiple-choice exam), they are worth looking into.

Audio.

Audio review CDs and MP3s are available from distinguished professors and bar review experts for most of the core classes. These experts provide, in 5 to 10 hours, a general overview of the entire topic, focusing mostly on the black letter law (the core legal points). They usually provide a little discussion of the holding of the most important cases and background on key statutes, but the primary emphasis is on the law and how to apply it to questions on your exams.

Thomson West publishes the *Sum & Substance* series on CD, which features a distinguished professor giving an organized lecture on all the major topics. They are usually pretty good, but can be costly—about $80 new if purchased on Amazon. com. Your bookstore might have some of these CDs for sale, but your best bet is probably to buy them online through a retailer like Amazon or on West's Web site. Some law libraries will have copies that you can check out, but the flexibility of having your own copy is worth it.

Do not give in to the temptation to steal or illegally copy the CDs. Even if you are sure you will not get caught, and even if you have a history of copying or downloading music illegally, you are in law school now and it is important to get in the habit of obeying the law. There are better ways to save money.

Kaplan PMBR has a set of CDs on all the first-year topics. They are now distributing it as CDs full of MP3s, although used copies of actual audio CDs are still being passed around some places. Although you can buy it, Kaplan gives these out for free to students who sign-up to take their bar review course after graduating (they ask you to put down a deposit as a 1L to lock-in your postgraduation price). Even if you do not want to pay a deposit to Kaplan, others at your school probably already have, so you can probably find a copy from a friend who is not using it. You might even be able to get a free copy from a Kaplan rep if you ask nice, but friends are usually a better bet. The Kaplan MP3s are actually designed for bar review prep, but the same elements for false imprisonment tested on the bar exam are usually tested on your torts exam. Ignore the bar-exam strategy material and listen to the law. The quality of each subject varies depending on the lecturer, from barely tolerable to exceptional. The contracts review from Professor Dan Fessler at U.C.

Davis is truly great. Unlike the *Sum & Substance* CDs, Kaplan will not have products available for more specialized upper-level courses (like Antitrust).

The Center for Computer Assisted Legal Instruction (CALI)'s Web site (www.cali.org) also makes available MP3 lectures and podcasts available for free to help law students. As I write this book, the selection is somewhat limited, but CALI is making a real effort to expand its offerings and it is worth checking out their Web site.

I was a big fan of audio supplements, but I did not use them for every class. After the first year, I only bought audio supplements for more difficult classes. Audio supplements can help you maximize your time by allowing you to study while driving, working out, or cleaning the apartment. If you have a long commute, it might be worth assembling audio supplements for every class. If you have little time where an audio supplement would be appropriate and you are an audio learner, consider picking one up for the class you find most difficult. Audio supplements are very general and helpful at building understanding for a class, which means that they are not particularly helpful at exam time (unless you are simply trying to squeeze law into every available minute and switching your playlist from "rap" to "real property in the gym" helps). The best way to use them is to listen through the entire supplement early in the semester to help cement the concepts and give you an understanding of the entire course.

Electronic study aids.

Aspen's *Study Desk* software allows you to access digital versions of their printed products on your computer. For some people, this may be the way to go. We are likely to see an increasing number of print books offered digitally, and of exclusively digital offerings.

CALI has a series of free modules on their Web site, organized by subject, with varying degrees of specialization—some get really technical and focused on small sub-sub-topics, which can be very helpful. These take about 15 minutes to 1 hour to complete. They start by showing you the law, then asking you to apply to a series of practice questions and other tests. If you already know the law on a subject and are simply looking for more practice questions, it can be kind of annoying to have to flip through the pages of their modules (it is not as easy as flipping to the back of a printed commercial outline), but the product is free and available for just about every class you can think of, so take a look.

Flash cards.

I loved using flash cards to study for law school. Aspen's *Law in a Flash* was the single best product I used in law school. Each box contains a few hundred flash cards (each one the size of a business card) for any given course but, unfortunately, *Law in a Flash* is not available for every subject, just the more popular ones.

The cards start by giving you the black-letter law on any given topic, and then ask you increasingly difficult fact patterns that eventually help you discover the exceptions to the rules and finer nuances of a subject. *Law in a Flash* is very well organized, and this organization allows you to work through the flash cards without knowing the material first—in other words, it both teaches the underlying law and helps you practice applying it to facts. In addition, I also liked the physical act of going through the flash cards, and that they are numbered. Crossing a certain threshold—finishing 25, 100, or the entire box—really gave me a sense of accomplishment and boosted my pride. I also liked their portability and could tuck a small group of cards in my shirt pocket to look at while waiting in line. My only critique is that sometimes *CrunchTime* uses a selection of the questions from *Law in a Flash* for its short-answer section, which reduced the value of *CrunchTime*.

I am aware that other companies make flash cards, like *Barron's First Year Law School Flashcards*. And while I have never known anyone who used them, the number of cards per topic and number of topics covered by Barron's makes *Law in a Flash* seem a lot more useful.

Some Lessons on Using Supplements

Study aids help you learn the law, which is what you are tested for on the final exam. The recommendations I make below, and the advice in the study aids themselves, are no substitute for your professor's instruction because you are being tested on the law according to your professor. Your class will likely cover less material than the commercial supplement—ignore the parts that cover topics not relevant to your class.

Make sure you learn your professor's wording and lingo. Try to learn any quirks about your professor's views, including whether he or she is simply wrong on a legal topic. If there is a disagreement between your professor and the treatise, check to make sure you correctly understand your professor's view, but go with your professor instead of the treatise. In other words, side with your professor's view rather than what you read in the treatise.

Supplements are valuable; use them.

Commercial supplements can be extremely valuable but will not do you any good if they sit on a shelf in your bedroom. Take the time to actually use them over the course of the semester. I always found that reading a short commercial outline (like the *CrunchTime* capsule summary) early in a semester will help to get my bearings for the course and the subject. Many people use supplements as a reference during the semester to look up things in the casebook or class they do not understand. This may be one of the best ways to use a supplement. A supplement can also help develop your outline and can help you make sure that what you are putting in your outline is legally correct.

Commercial supplements also give you practice exams and model answers. These are not as good as having practice exams and answers from your professors, but rarely will you be fortunate to get enough sample questions with answers from your professors. Doing practice questions, at least in the period leading up to finals, can be very helpful. Some supplements include explicit exam pointers, which tell you the areas that professors are most likely to test on and how to get the most points in that subject. These recommendations may not match your individual professor, but they could still be helpful.

Supplements also present different time options. You can do a few flash cards at a time or answer some multiple-choice questions or read an outline on the topic of negligence if you have a small window of free time. It is very hard to read through a big case in a casebook in 15 minutes.

Identify big issues and weaknesses.

One of the big disadvantages of having a typical law school final at the end of the semester is that you have no idea how well you are doing in the class. Taking practice questions in commercial supplements can give you a warning if you are struggling with a subject or a specific topic in that subject. If you find a question difficult, mark it up so you can come back to it later. If you find a particular flash card difficult, separate it from the box so you can study it repeatedly. And if you find some wording in a treatise or outline super helpful or super confusing, write on it and come back to it later. These products are designed to be used.

Diversity can help.

Although many students prefer having just one supplement, I liked to have multiple ones on any given topic. It allowed me to change which one I was studying from over the course of the semester. I did not like to re-read the same material because my mind would sometimes skip around and miss words. Seeing a concept worded or explained in different ways was also very helpful to me. The more examples, analogies, and explanations I encountered, the better I was able to see the unifying theme and concept.

One thing I struggled with was identifying when a set of facts meant that probable cause existed for Fourth Amendment purposes. Practice questions helped me to realize that my instincts and intuition were completely off base. I would look at a set of facts and think there is no way this reaches the level of probable cause only to see the Supreme Court had said otherwise. Then, in response, I would swing too far in the other direction. Seeing probable cause and the fact patterns giving rise to it explained differently allowed me to do well on the final exam. Some folks, on the other hand, would instead be confused by seeing the same thing worded differently.

A diversity of testing methods can also help. Many testing aids include short answer, multiple choice, true/false questions, and the like. Even if your final exam is completely essay based, these quicker-to-answer questions can still help. You can get through them and hit more concepts more quickly. They are not substitutes for practicing essay-style questions, but they can still help.

Pick the supplements based on, and tailor their use to, your learning styles.

One supplement is not necessarily better than another, but it may be better for you. I am the type of reader who tries to skip around in a paragraph to find the material I need. I do not need a lot of connectors and I like to move quickly through material because I get bored easily. Commercial outlines work better for me than prose and treatises. Others would value the paragraph form more. I learn well from audio and can pay attention to audio CDs while driving; some people just tune them out.

How you use the supplements can also be adjusted to your learning style. Flash cards, for example, can be done with friends. This was not my style, but I know others did it. As a 3L, I tutored a couple groups of first years in torts. I would bring them into my law journal's office and go through some *Law in a Flash* cards I had preselected as having complicated fact patterns with debatable answers. They seemed to enjoy discussing and figuring out the answer as a group. A group approach can also work for some of the essay questions contained in testing aids, but probably does not work with audio books.

I also enjoyed feeling a sense of progress. In addition to plowing through flash cards, checking off that I had finished reading a supplement or a part of a supplement made me feel great. It is a constant struggle to keep up with the daily grind of law school. Finishing an outline is a momentous tax. Sometimes it feels nice to be able to just finish something—even if it is listening to an audio CD.

Experiment and evaluate.

Just like everything else in this book, it is important to find what works for you. I strongly encourage you to experiment with commercial supplements to find what works for you. Even if your professor talks you out of looking at a heretical commercial outline, get a testing aid with some practice questions in it. Figure out what product works for you and reject products that do not.

As explained earlier, I really liked *CrunchTime* and *Law in a Flash*. *CrunchTime* often borrowed short-answer questions from *Law in a Flash*, which really annoyed me when I got to that section. However, I continued buying *CrunchTime* because the writing style really worked for me and I liked the size, shape, and even binding of the book. It was smaller than other products and I liked that. It made it more portable and it fit better on the bar-style counters at which I often studied. I was also pretty rough with my books, and *CrunchTime's* binding seemed to fair better than the competition when I tried using other products. This is a pretty trivial reason to use a product, but it worked for me. I would encourage you to look at or try new products until you find what fits your style and needs.

Chapter 5

WRITING A LAW SCHOOL EXAM

BY THIS POINT, YOU SHOULD REALIZE HOW IMPORTANT THE LAW SCHOOL EXAM IS. Learning the law to be able to give a right answer is very important, but writing the answer well is also important. It is so important that entire books are written just about writing the exam itself, like *Getting to Maybe*, which is 348 pages long. This chapter is not nearly that long, but it covers the basics of doing well on an exam. As a successful graduate recently explained to me, the two keys to acing a law exam are 1) saying what the law professor wants you to say and 2) stringing the words together well. If you can regurgitate exactly what your law professor wants and regurgitate it well, you are golden.

Knowing What to Say
Read the Question Carefully

The only way to get the question right is to answer the right question. One of my friends recently recounted what happened to a classmate in a criminal law exam. The professor gave an interesting fact pattern involving a terrorist hijacker and a brave passenger who fought and killed the hijacker but was unable to land the plane, and it crashed. I assume the inspiration came from United 93, which crashed in Pennsylvania on September 11, 2001. The call of the question—the last part, which instructs students—asked students to analyze what crimes the *passenger* committed and what defenses he might have.

Obviously, the passenger who bravely fought the hijacker but was unable to save the day would have some pretty decent defenses. The student misread the question and thought it was about what crimes the *hijacker* committed and what defenses would be available to him. The answer was completely wrong because it did not even identify the right issues (mostly defenses rather than crimes) to address. This student had straight As except for this exam. Do not let this happen to you. Identify actors and circle or underline their names. Flag game-changing modifiers such as "un" or "not." If you face a fairly long fact pattern, it can be helpful to read the call of the question at the very bottom first, then read then fact pattern, then read the call of the question again. Had this student first read the question and identified that he should be focused on the passenger and not the hijacker, he probably would have aced this exam too.

Spot the Issues

The only way to get points on an exam is to spot the issues raised by the question. Sometimes the question will be very clear and ask you to analyze one specific issue, but many times you will have to spot the issue yourself. Start from the call of the question and work your way through the facts.

With the hijacker–passenger example, you are being instructed to focus on one actor and his crimes and defenses. You do not need to analyze other actors' crimes, unless they tie into the passenger's crimes and defenses. Start by looking for the transactions. Comb through the facts and look for transactions. The passenger killed the hijacker. That is a transaction. What crimes did he commit by doing this? What defenses are available to him? Crashing the plane and killing the others would be a transaction. If he shoved a flight attendant while charging the hijacker, that would be a transaction, too. In fact patterns of this nature, it is helpful to break down each transaction and each issue raised in each transaction.

Once you have identified the transactions, apply each of the legal issues to the transaction at issue. In torts and criminal law, this would probably include running through a mental list of all the torts and crimes you covered in class to see if any apply. In a contracts class, this would include recognizing that a problematic offer, counteroffer, and acceptance situation raises questions about both contract formation and the terms of the contracts. Focus on each line of the fact pattern to identify the facts that raise legal issues.

Answer with the Correct Law According to Your Professor

This one is really simple. Answer with the modern law according to your professor. Unless you're explicitly told to answer with outdated law, use modern law. Historical issues that may be interesting to you are simply not relevant here. If a case was overruled, do not use that line of precedent unless asked. If a case on civil rights is set a hundred years ago, you should mention the separate but equal doctrine. But unless you are told otherwise, assume modern law applies and do not explain how a different result would have been reached before *Brown v. Board of Education.*

Your professor is the one grading your exam. He or she is right. If you think the law is wrong, that does not matter. This is not the place to criticize the law or suggest that the law should be different. You may face a policy question that calls for a policy answer, but that is addressed in a different chapter. Here, your job is to describe the law as your professor thinks the law is. This may be different from the policy your professor likes. If you have a liberal professor who criticizes the U.S. Supreme Court as being too conservative and pro-police when it comes to the Fourth Amendment, this does not mean you should give a liberal answer. The fact that your professor has a policy preference for a robust Fourth Amendment does not mean that your professor believes the current modern law is as liberal as her views.

Show the Importance of Facts Known and Unknown

A law school exam is not a pure test on the law. You are not asked to write out the legal rules or explain them, you are asked to apply them to the fact pattern provided by your professor. This requires you to identify the relevant facts and explain how they are relevant in light of the governing law. When going through the fact pattern, underline or circle the facts that matter. Take notes on the fact pattern, and then explain why these things matter.

For example, assume you face a fact pattern involving self-defense in a jurisdiction where a reasonable mistake of fact justifies the mistaken act. If the fact pattern states that the defendant saw a metallic object in the victim's hand, that is something to note. If it was dark outside when this happened, that is something to note. If the defendant had personal knowledge that the victim was prone to carrying a gun around, that was something to note. After explaining the rule that a reasonable mistake that the victim was carrying a gun would permit self-defense even though the victim only had a toy, you would then work in the facts that tend to show the mistake was reasonable—that the toy was metallic, that it was dark out, that the defendant knew the victim often carried a gun. Then you would evaluate these facts and conclude whether or not this likely constitutes a reasonable mistake. Along the way, you would explain which facts are the most important.

Sometimes discussing facts that are not provided is even more important. If the fact pattern says that Sam shot Bill in the dark and Sam claims it was self-defense—with nothing more—you would have to discuss and evaluate the facts required to reach a conclusion. This is not to suggest that you should start inserting hypothetical facts into every question. When a detail is intentionally left out by your professor, it is because he or she wants you to discuss the differences the detail would make. The same is true of law. If you learned a majority and a minority rule (different laws in different jurisdictions) and you are not told which to apply, you need to discuss the different possible outcomes based on the different legal principles.

This can be approached by putting together a decision tree of "if-then" statements. Assume a fact pattern where a bystander walks up on two people fighting. The bystander sees one person pull a knife. He draws his gun and shoots the person holding the knife. It turns out the knife-puller was an undercover police officer who had, moments earlier, taken the knife from the dangerous criminal she was fighting with.

If this jurisdiction follows the majority rule, then the "defense of others" defense applies if the shooter made a reasonable mistake in shooting the officer. Then you would discuss the facts in a similar set of if-then statements showing which facts would make the mistake reasonable and which ones would not.

If this jurisdiction follows the minority rule, then the shooter "steps into the shoes" of the criminal the officer was fighting with and is only justified in shooting the officer if the criminal would have been justified to do so. Here you would discuss a different set of facts—which ones might have made it justifiable to shoot the officer. You would discuss concepts such as excessive force. The two different legal tests require different facts to reach different conclusions. If well-written, the if-then pattern should flow better and show the professor that you understand the distinctions and know what really matters.

Evaluate Arguments and Legal Issues

Sometimes a question calls for an easy answer. The defendant is guilty or not guilty. That does not make for a very hard exam, though. Easy answers are usually only found as a part of a bigger answer. The defendant faces possible conviction of a dozen crimes. The battery charge is easy; the question is whether he can face a conviction for felony murder. When faced with a typically difficult law school question, the proper course is to evaluate each argument. One side may be stronger than the other, and you should admit as much and explain why. But often times it will be a close call, and you will not have enough facts to answer definitively. This is why the book on exam writing is called *Getting to Maybe*. Keep that in mind.

Saying It Well

The better you are at writing in general, the easier writing a law exam will be. These tips are focused on some of the unique issues you face in a law exam.

Say It the Way You Are Supposed to Say It

Most essay exams will explain your audience. Are you writing a memo to a partner at your firm? Are you an advocate making the strongest possible case for your client? Identify your audience and act accordingly. If you are an advocate, pick the best arguments why your client should win. Acknowledge the other side's arguments and respond to them—do not say they are right. If you are asked to provide a more neutral analysis, evaluate all of the arguments. If you are not instructed one way or the other, assume this a legal memo and evaluate all of the arguments.

Say What You Are Supposed to Say

Answer the question. It really is that simple. Every semester, though, some students greatly annoy their professors by just not answering the question. They write what they want to write or just tweak the question. This is not a mistake in reading the question, it is an outright refusal to follow it. This is not a good idea.

Do not argue that the prevailing law is wrong or bring up irrelevant historical details. Just because you learn something in class about *Marbury v. Madison* or the *real* nature of the administrative state, you do not have to write a paragraph about it in response to a simple question. A little common sense goes a long way in this regard.

Say It in the Right Order with the Right Format (IRAC)

Write your exam in the IRAC format. If you have already started law school, you might have heard this mentioned as if it is such a hard and complicated thing. It is not. First you cover the *issue*, then you cover the *rule*, then you *analyze* the facts, then you write a *conclusion*. In a super-simple and crude form:

> **Issue:** The first issue raised is whether a contract was formed.
>
> **Rule:** Contract formation requires a "meeting of the minds." This requires an offer and an acceptance of the offer before it expired.
>
> **Analysis:** Here, the facts tell us that the offer required acceptance via e-mail and stated, "This offer expires at midnight." Sam forgot to set his watch ahead an hour due to the Daylight Savings Time switch and thought he accepted the offer before midnight. By its own terms, the offer had expired before Sam accepted it.
>
> **Conclusion:** Because the offer had expired, no contract was formed.

This is a very crude example, and as I wrote it I was already thinking of ways Sam might try to enforce the deal. Normally you would not want to put actual headings that say "Issue," "Rule," "Analysis," and "Conclusion." I include these only to illustrate the kind of language that can be found in each section. The transition between rule and analysis often makes for a natural paragraph break. Putting some kind of transition, break, or spacing between sections helps to highlight them for the professor.

Show Your Work

A law school exam tests you on your application of law to facts, not necessarily on your conclusions. You do not gain any points by regurgitating the facts from the question. You gain points by showing which facts matter and which facts do not. Regurgitating the law may be somewhat helpful, but applying it is the most important. Skipping the application process, or failing to show the professor how you applied the law, will hurt you.

In my IRAC example above, cutting out the analysis would cost me points. If I stated the rule that an offer must be accepted before it expires and then said there was no contract here, I would get fewer points than if I explained that the offer was accepted late. Just as with an algebra problem, showing your work is the only way for the professor to know you used the right method to get the conclusion.

Avoid Superlatives and Absolutes

Do not use words like clearly, obviously, or certainly unless it really is clear, obvious, or certain. If your professor put it on the exam, it probably is not clear, obvious, or certain. Quite frankly, saying that something is clear, obvious, or certain usually undermines your argument. If the defendant is clearly guilty, you probably would not have to *tell* me that he is clearly guilty, your argument and facts would *show* it quite easily. When providing neutral analysis, a little "maybe" can be helpful. Instead of saying he is unquestionably guilty, you could say that he would likely be found guilty. It might be better to describe an argument as the best argument rather than as the correct argument.

Make It Nice

As your professors go through a large stack of exams, anything you can do to make it easier for them to give you points is appreciated. After my first semester I made a point of visiting each of my professors to talk about what they liked about my exam. This is a good habit to get into. My property exam was interesting. It was difficult, but it was short. Many people finished early. As an undergrad, I was fully content to leave an exam early. In law school, it seemed wrong. I finished with more than an hour and a half left (at least one student had already left). I decided to spend the remaining time formatting my exam.

I put in great headings and subheadings, with the headings bolded and subheadings italicized and sub-subheadings underlined. I mostly did this because I refused to leave the exam that early. But when I met with the property professor afterward, he praised the formatting. He explained how it made it easy to read and grade the exam. In hindsight, this makes perfect sense to me. When I write a brief to a judge, I use all sorts of formatting, headings, and subheadings to help her rule in my favor. Of course, I usually do not write briefs in a three-hour closed-book session. Do not think about formatting until you are completely done and satisfied with your answer. If you are completely finished early, then use the extra time to make the answer look better.

Before messing with formatting, review your answer and proofread it. Generally spelling and grammar will not be counted against you if the software lacks spell-check, but poor spelling certainly does not help you.

Do Not Screw Up
Do Not Panic

If you panic, try to calm down. Realize everything on the exam was covered in the class you took. There is nothing on the exam you have not heard and read before at least once, maybe a dozen times. If there is another question to answer, start with that. If you are stuck on a tough question, start with the biggest topic you can and work your way to specific subtopics. Write the part of the rule you do know and keep going until something comes back to you.

If You Run Out of Time

Some experts recommend outlining an answer in your bluebook before writing it. Some kind of outline is always helpful in developing structure. The idea of doing it in your bluebook is that, if you completely run out of time, you will have some answer in place that will signal to your professor that you know the answer. This makes some sense, but I would encourage you to manage your time better to avoid a total collapse.

If you are running out of time, keep in mind that the R and A—Rule and Analysis—is more important than the I and C—Issue and Conclusion—when it comes to getting points. If you have only two minutes to answer a question, do not worry about teeing up the issue. Do not simply write "Defendant wins." Spend your limited time in framing the legal rule and the analysis that requires the application of the law to the facts. This is the big thing your professor is looking for—not who wins, but that you know and know how to apply the law.

Find Your Strengths and Weaknesses, and Deal with Them

One of my strengths was short-term memory. I could repeat things in my head and type them into the bluebook as soon as an exam started. With contracts, where I thought having a road map would help, I spent the lead-up to the exam focusing on keeping that road map in my memory. As soon as the exam started, I typed it into the electronic bluebook, and then I looked at the question. In my property exam, the professor believed that learning case names was important. He would give us one point for every case name we legitimately cited. I committed a list of twenty case names to my short-term memory and typed them into the bluebook before starting the exam. Others had entirely different strengths to play to.

Some people are very good at creating and remembering mnemonics, patterns of letters or phrases that have some meaning. Math fans use "How I need a drink, alcoholic of course, after the tough lectures involving quantum mechanics" to remember the value of pi. If you count the number of letters in each word, the result is 3.14159265358979. I heard about a young woman who was stellar at creating mnemonics and did quite well with them. One of my friends studied with her for a class and she shared a series of lurid, sex-based mnemonics she had created. Although he could never come up functional mnemonics on his own, he was able to remember every word of her mnemonics. He did well on that exam. The point here is that you should try to think about your skills.

Figuring out your weaknesses is just as important. If I overthink the spelling of a word, I end up spelling it wrong. The word *likely* for some reason creates weird problems for me. Is it one L or two? I used *likely* a lot on exams: "Sam likely has a cause of action against Pete." Because this word threw me off, I learned to check how to spell it before starting an exam. Most of you can probably spell *likely*, but you may have your own struggles—physical, mental, or emotional. The key thing is to be honest with yourself and take steps to reduce their impact.

Key Points

- The key to acing a law exam are to know what the professor wants you to say and to string the words together well.
- Read the question carefully and answer the right question.
- Flag game changing modifiers like "un" or "not."
- Spot the issues, look for transactions, and find how they relate in answering the question presented.
- Answer with the correct modern law (unless explicitly told otherwise).
- Your professor is right. Answer the way your professor would since he or she is the one grading your exam.
- Explain why relevant facts matter.
- If you learned a majority and a minority rule and you are not told which to apply, discuss the outcomes of both using if-then patterns to demonstrate concise and full understanding of the issues and distinctions.
- Avoid superlatives or absolutes.
- Don't panic.
- Write in the IRAC format. If you run out of time, keep in mind that the R and A in the IRAC is more important than the I and C when it comes to getting points, so focus accordingly. Your professor is looking to see that you know and apply the law, not just know who wins.
- Work with your strengths and weaknesses.

Chapter 6

VARIATIONS: MULTIPLE-CHOICE, TRUE/FALSE, SHORT-ANSWER, POLICY-QUESTION, OPEN-BOOK, TAKE-HOME, AND PASS/FAIL EXAMS

THE MOST COMMON TYPE OF LAW SCHOOL EXAM is the typical issue-spotter essay in which you are given a lengthy fact pattern and a broad call of the question. Sometimes, you get something different. One of my professors included multiple-choice, true/false, essay, and short-answer questions all on the same exam. He explained that he was not sure what was the best way to test on law; certain methods seemed to benefit some students more than others, and he was still in search of the fairest, most accurate way to test our learning. You will likely have advance warning on the types of questions that will be on your exams, and so you should prepare accordingly.

Multiple-Choice Questions

Some professors will use multiple-choice questions on their exams, as either the primary means of testing or a small part of the exam. I had three exams with multiple-choice components:

- **Civ Pro.** The questions were super easy and appeared just to verify that I had memorized the simple material. The questions were *very* similar to the sample prior year's questions the professor had provided and counted for only 5 percent of the exam.
- **Corporations.** These multiple-choice questions were insanely hard and still hurt my head. The exam also featured a tough essay. To teach us a point about expectant value, the professor partially penalized us for getting wrong answers. The questions were not necessarily tricky; it was the subject matter and scope of the questions that made them hard. They were fit for long essays that concluded with "maybe" rather than definitive multiple-choice answers.
- **Criminal Procedure**. I took this class during my last semester. Some of the questions were very hard, in the style of Multistate Bar Examination. They were tricky. Others were quite easy, and everyone was clumped together close on the curve. This made a handful of questions determinative of the entire exam. This class included a midterm that was almost entirely multiple-choice and a final that had a mix of just about every type of question imaginable.

Each of these exams was quite different, but they all required me to use a slightly different strategy than I used with essay exams.

Strategy

The most important strategy suggestion I have is to use one when taking the test. If you aced the LSAT, you probably have a solid multiple-choice strategy to use. But the rest of us need to take multiple-choice tests seriously, swallow our pride, and take concrete steps to get better results. Circle the call of the question. Underline the actors so you know that the question asks whether Tommy is guilty of battery rather than Randy. Underline game-changing words like *not* in the question. And cross out answers you know are wrong to narrow your choices. These are simple things that you have probably heard before, but make sure you actually use them.

Time management can also get more interesting in tests that involve both essays and multiple-choice questions. If you spend too much time oscillating between answers A and B, you might not have enough time for the essay. If you work away at the essay until it is perfect, you might not have enough time if the multiple-choice questions are hard. Make a conscious effort to manage your time.

My time-management strategy involved doing the multiple-choice questions first. I got the "easiest" questions out of the way. Any question that was too hard for me I just marked the answer down right away and left it for later, drawing a star next to it. Then I went on to the essay with a sense of how many tough multiple-choice questions I would have to go back to and how much time that might take. This worked for me because my mind can switch gears easily between questions. This would not work for everyone. Just mind the time, leave room for the essays, and do not shortchange the multiple-choice.

Studying for Multiple-Choice Exams

Your study plans for an exam with multiple-choice questions should include doing multiple-choice questions. Even if your professor makes some questions available, they probably will not be enough. See Chapter 4's coverage of commercial supplements for a discussion of which products include multiple-choice questions. Practice some of your test-taking strategies (e.g., crossing off wrong answers) on these practice questions, too.

As I mentioned before, my criminal procedure professor used some tricky questions on the final exam. After the midterm grades came out, it was clear that most students did pretty well. We were very bunched together on the curve, with only a few points separating an A from a B. I was just above average and on track for a B+. I really wanted an A but needed to get all or almost all of the final exam questions right to pull it off, which meant getting all the tricky questions right. Because I was taking two other classes pass/fail, I had the opportunity to really go crazy on preparing for the multiple-choice exam.

In addition to doing the multiple-choice questions in supplements I already had, I bought a whole book of practice multiple-choice questions on criminal procedure. These were helpful but not quite tricky enough. I had just received my practice workbooks for the bar exam in the mail, so I turned to the Kaplan PMBR criminal-procedure practice questions. The bar review questions covered topics that my class did not, but the book had a topical index, so I could avoid taking questions on topics not covered in class. With both of these sets of questions, I flagged the ones I got wrong, which tended to be the tricky questions. I took those questions again later until I got them right twice in a row. I made a written list of reasons that I got the question wrong—which tricks I fell for. I mastered not just the law but the test, and I got an A.

That was probably overkill. I would not recommend using bar review questions to prepare for law school exams. But it worked well to dig me out of a hole. If I had done more practice questions to prepare myself for the midterm, I probably would not have needed to do as much for the final.

True/False Questions

True/false questions are not confined to grade school. Though less common than other kinds of questions, they might get thrown at you as a part of an exam. You will usually know ahead of time. True/false questions may sound easy, but they are *not* necessarily easy. As with multiple-choice questions, they can be easy, throwaway questions used to make sure you understand a simple point or they can be real hard. As always, you should look at your professor's old exams (if available) to see what kind of questions he or she asks and to practice answering them. You can also find practice true/false questions in commercial supplements, which are covered in Chapter 4. If you are unsure about whether a supplement includes true/false questions, take a look at it in the library or bookstore before buying. You can also use the preview option on Amazon.com to look inside some books before making a purchase.

True/false questions will likely fall into two basic categories: easy, throwaway questions that everyone gets right and are designed to simply make sure you understand the material, and very hard and tricky questions. The former you do not need to worry about; the latter take effort. Tricky true/false questions tend to really probe your thinking and knowledge of the issue. If you are warned that true/false questions might be on the exam, be prepared for tricky questions, unless you have reason to believe that the questions will be easy. With tricky true/false questions, you have to be able to spot issues, even detached from facts.

Approach each question with strategy. Read it clearly, underline it or make notes as appropriate, and keep any double negatives straight. If it includes double negatives ("not unconstitutional"), consider rewriting it in a clear way next to the question. There is a fine line between overthinking and appropriately studying a question. First, I try to see if the question seems true. Then I try to falsify it. I think of any possible way the question could be false. Then I pause to consider whether my idea of how it is false is reasonable—I ask myself whether this is what the professor could possibly be getting at with the question. In other words, I ask myself whether I am overthinking it.

My criminal procedure professor included some very difficult true/false questions on his exam. I cannot remember the toughest ones, but here is an example of a standard question. During our class, the professor had taught us that racial discrimination was not a violation of constitutional criminal procedure under the Fourth Amendment and did not trigger the Fourth Amendment's exclusionary rule. The question was something like this:

> **With probable cause to believe that a crime was committed, a police officer pulled over a black man because he was black. The Constitution was not violated. True or false?**

Now, this almost seems true because we learned that the Fourth Amendment is not violated by racial profiling, and here we are told that there was probable cause that some crime was committed. But the statement is false because such profiling violates the Equal Protection Clause. I started to wonder, though, whether it was nevertheless true. If the officer had probable cause to pull him over anyway, then was the individual actually harmed? If there was no harm, is there a constitutional violation? But this was overthinking the question. What my professor was getting at is that, even though the officer did not violate the constitutional protections for criminals, he violated the Equal Protection Clause. To answer this question correctly, students needed to think critically and remember that a constitutional violation still existed (even if it had no apparent remedy), rather than remember feeling angry in class when learning that the evidence obtained from such a search could be used against the criminal defendant. But it was equally important not to overthink the question and give the answer the professor was looking for.

Short-Answer Questions

Short-answer questions require nothing more than a short essay. A smaller fact pattern makes it easier to spot issues and makes it hard for the professor to include numerous or complicated issues. If you get such a question, your professor is testing whether you can discuss this easy-to-spot issue. Identify what the professor wants and answer the question. Do not overwrite or overanalyze something that is designed for a quick, short answer. For example, if your constitutional law class short-answer question presents a fact pattern that lines up with existing Supreme Court precedent, just answer the question and invoke the case—do not explain why the case is wrong or what Justice Thomas would think *unless asked to do so.*

Policy Questions

Policy questions do not include a fact pattern and are much more subjective than a typical law-school-exam essay question. In a way, these questions are more like undergrad liberal arts exams. A policy question can range from asking why contracts require consideration or what are the reasons behind the consideration rule to requiring you to take a position on or debate an issue to a full-blown policy question that asks you how to fix a significant public policy problem.

You are less likely to encounter policy questions than issue-spotters. If you do face policy questions, they are likely to be relatively short and count for 5 to 20 percent of your exam. Your professor may tell you if a policy question is coming. But even if you are not explicitly warned, you should pay attention to policy discussions in class. If your torts professor talks about tort reform ideas and the Coase theorem, you may face a policy question on tort reform. You should be mentally prepared for a policy question no matter what, though, just in case your professor surprises you with one. And if you hate being surprised, go ahead and ask your professor if he or she plans on including policy questions on the exam.

How to Prepare

Personally, I hate super-subjective questions like these. How do you study for something that essentially asks your opinion? These questions, in part, test your BSing skills. This might please many law students, or at least those with a liberal arts background, but could scare engineers. Gunners who want the top grade might be particularly worried about a question that cannot be studied for in the same way the rule of perpetuities can be. Do not let these questions freak you out.

You should always try to understand the policies behind the cases or doctrines you study in class. This will be of great importance on policy questions, but understanding the "why" behind the law can also help you make an informed guess on a legal question that you do not know the answer to. When your professor offers policy analysis in class, be sure to take notes on and study it. Once again, understanding how your professor thinks is critical if a policy question comes up, but it will also help you know what he or she is trying to get at in normal legal questions. Similarly, looking at law review articles authored by your professor (at least skimming the introduction, proposal, and conclusion sections) can give you insight on both the policy issues and your professor's thoughts on them.

One of the best ways to prepare for policy questions is to simply talk about the issues. Debating and discussing policy issues with your classmates over the course of the semester can be very beneficial. If your torts class discusses various tort reforms, talk about them with your classmates outside of class. Are you most sympathetic to injured plaintiffs or businesses facing frivolous lawsuits? Which ideas for reform do you like the most? Which do you hate? The experience of discussing issues outside of class will help you to understand the issues better as you learn arguments and counterarguments for your peers, make it easier for you to take a personal position on the exam, and get you in the habit of articulating policy positions. Finally, you can prepare for policy questions by simply staying informed and reading the news. You may very well be facing a policy question that is ripped from the headlines. Your professor is staying informed about what is going on in the world, but many law students—especially 1Ls—are so overwhelmed with school that they don't take the time to stay informed. If you take a little time to read the news and put a little mental energy into thinking about the legal issues inherent in the articles you see, you will gain additional practice with policy issues and might get lucky enough to have actually read and thought about the issue you face on the exam.

Writing a Policy Question

Just because a policy question is very subjective and squishy does not mean you treat it differently than a normal essay question when it comes to your initial approach. Take some time to think about it and organize your answer before writing. And if you did not study for the policy question or have no idea what it is even getting at, do not freak out; simply reread the question and try to figure it out. The basic approach is to make your argument and deal with counterarguments.

If you have paid attention to or investigated your professor, you may have a good idea of what position he or she would take on the issue in the question. Whether to simply agree with the professor can be a tough call, and this depends in part on your personal ethics. Of course, professors will tell you that they grade objectively and without personal bias, but they too are human. Most times it is probably better to agree with your professor, unless you know how to argue the other side of the question substantially better. I heard a story, though, about a student that this backfired on. She was the lone conservative in an environmental law class and was vocal about her positions during class discussion. The professor was a liberal. The student was used to getting excellent grades and took advantage of the fact that her exam was blind-graded to take a liberal position on the policy question (this one counted for the majority of the exam) and win the A. But she ended up with a low grade. Apparently, when the professor realized that all of his students had taken a liberal position, he docked the conservative student for taking a position that she had disagreed with in class. This is a rare situation, and the story might not even be true, but I think it highlights the risk of being too strategic when facing a policy question.

Open-Book Exams

Open-book exams, in which you are allowed to consult outside resources during the exam, are very common at some schools and unheard-of at others. Professors might limit you to your casebook and outlines or notes you made yourself. They might let you bring in commercial supplements. And I have even heard of professors permitting students to do legal research online—so long as they did not chat or communicate with each other. There are two important points to remember on open-book exams:

1. Open-book exams are not necessarily easier. You are being graded on a curve, and everybody else is getting the same advantage.
2. You have the same amount of time as on a closed-book exam and are simply not going to have a chance to do much with the open book itself.

What to Bring to an Open-Book Exam; What to Use with an Open-Book Exam

What should you bring to an open-book exam? Everything. As a student I believed in only *using* a few things during the exam but *bringing* everything that has even the slimmest possibility of being useful. What did it hurt me to have a commercial supplement on the floor next to my desk? Even if I did not look at it once during the exam, if I already owned the book, it did not cost me any time or money to bring it there. I deviated from this policy once, and I still regret it.

My Federal Antitrust professor made a comment at some point during the semester that jumped out at me. He said that health care was the big field in antitrust law these days and the Department of Justice had a really specific set of antitrust guidelines to apply just in the health care field. I think he praised those guidelines, but whatever he said, it made me make a note to print them out from the DOJ Web site and have them with me at the exam. Shortly before the exam I went to print the guidelines. The printer in the student lounge broke. I was annoyed at the idea of having to walk 250 yards to another printer and just said, screw it—what was the chance I would need the guidelines? Sure enough, one of the final exam questions was a on a health care antitrust issue. If I had had those guidelines under my desk, I would have been able to pull them up and give the perfect answer. I would have faced the ethical dilemma of whether to cite the specific guideline I was using and tip the professor off to the fact that I had a copy with me or to just give the perfect answer that lined up with the set of guidelines he was undoubtedly using to grade the exam. This was the only exam I got an A— on in all of law school. I am still convinced that I should have brought everything that could possibly have been useful. But for every exam, just because I brought a stack of stuff does not mean that I used everything in the sack.

Usually the best thing to have with you and use is your own outline. By exam time you should be very familiar with your outline and know exactly where to find material on it. I was never big on using traditional outlines, and I wanted something smaller for exams. Whenever I had an open-book exam, I prepared a few pages of reference material to help me. Figures 2 and 3 are things I created for my open-book evidence exam.

Figure 1 is just a list of the Federal Rules of Evidence, arranged by number and with a description of the rule that jogs my memory. "Past molestation" might not mean much to you and does not mean anything to me now, but in law school it was enough to jog my memory of F.R.E. 414(a): "In a criminal case in which the defendant is accused of an offense of child molestation, evidence of the defendant's commission of another offense or offenses of child molestation is admissible, and may be considered for its bearing on any matter to which it is relevant." Having the rule numbers handy on this one-page sheet also allowed me to easily cite all the rules involved in my essay. I am not sure that it really helped my grade to have citations behind my answers, but it could not have hurt. The list of rules also served as a helpful checklist. Evidence exams tend to be full of hearsay and possible hearsay. Students need to figure out any possible way the evidence could be admissible. This rule list gave me an easy-to-access list of all the hearsay exceptions and exclusions.

Figure 3 consists of a series of notes that meant something to me at the time and seemed important enough to include for the exam. I had boiled down all my notes for the semester and all the material I thought I needed to these two pages. First, you will see that I put together a road map. Based on what my professor covered in class, I believed that every question should address those issues. You will also see that I included some phrases that the professor had used and liked, such as "rank hearsay," "a brick is not a wall," and the thing about a dead fish in milk. I even included a Bible quote I had heard in church. I knew the professor was a part-time pastor and thought it might come in handy. I did not end up using it since it seemed over-the-top.

Figure 2

102 Purpose and construction

103 Harm / error / need to object / offer proof

104 Preliminary fact finding, judge & jury

105 Jury limiting instruction

106 Admitting rest of doc or recording in fairness

201 Judicial notice

301 Presumptions

401 Relevancy defined

403 Exclusion of relevant evidence for prejudice, waste, or confusion

404 Character evidence (a) generally and (b) bad acts

405 Methods of proving character
   (a) reputation or opinion or specific questions on cross
   (b) specific instances when char is essential

406 Habit

407 Subsequent remedial measures

408 Offer to compromise

409 Offer to pay medical expenses

410 Pleas & offers to plea

411 Proof of insurance

412 Rape shield

413 Past rapes

414 Past molestation

415 Past rape & molestation in civil cases

501 Privileges – common law

601 Competency & <u>witnesses</u>

602 Personal knowledge

603 Oath

607 Impeach – anyone

608 Character of witness

609 Conviction evidence

612 Refreshing recollection

613 Prior statement impeachment (b) chance to respond

701 Opinion by lay

702 Expert opinion

703 Basis of expert opinion

704 Ultimate issue

705 Underlying data of expert

801 (c) defines hearsay
   (d) exclusions from hearsay:
   prior inconsistent statements made at a proceeding (oath) and subject to cross now prior consistent statement subject to cross now to rebut bias / fabrication admission by party opponent identification

803 Availability okay ( )
   1. present sense impression
   2. excited utterance
   3. then existing mental, emotional, physical condition
   4. statement for medical diagnosis
   5. recorded recollection
   6. business records
   7. absence of biz record
   8. public records and reports
   9. records of vital statistics
   10. absence of public record
   11. records of religious orgs about marriage, etc.
   12. marriage or baptismal certificates
   13. family records
   14. deeds / property recs
   15. statements in deeds
   16. ancient documents
   17. market reports
   18. learned treatises
   19. familial reputation
   20. community boundaries
   21. reputation as to character
   22. previous conviction
   23. judgments of history

804 Witness unavailable (a) defines unavailable (b):
   1. Former testimony (or deposition) w/ cross
   2. Dying declaration
   3. Statement against interest
   4. Personal / family history
   6. Forfeiture by wrongdoing

806 Can criticize credibility of out of court hearsay declarant as if was testify

807 Residual / catch-all exception

901 Authentication rules

1001 Definition of documents

1002 BER

1003 Duplicates admissible

1004-1007 Spec. doc rules

1008 Judge & jury roles w/ docs

Figure 3. Fed. R. Evid. # Road map

Voir dire / outside of jury

Foundation (of witness knowledge or exception) / authentication (stipulation)

Relevance – what is it offered to prove, does it, then 403? Other routes to admissibility? Go around not through the forbidden box.

Reliability – hearsay – definitional – what offered to prove

Catch-all

Confrontation (Crawford problem)

Limiting instruction

Basics

Motion in limine

Make sure you object!

System justifications

Harmless error doctrine on appeal is one of the most important parts of evidence

"French rule"

Foundation - remember f for hsay exceptions

Proponent of evidence has **burden** of proof regarding its admissibility. **Judicial notice** can help with authentication, can't bring in physical evidence without authentication

Privileges keep out a lot of evidence for policy, not reliability. Discovery easier than admissibility. Privilege can conflict with a right. Privilege only waived intentionally, not accidentally, but how you treat it suggests it was never privileged to begin with.

Analyze opinion testimony both ways – as lay or as expert when from experience. Tech or sci. gatekeeper. **daubert** factors

Empirical testing: theory, technique must be falsifiable, testable. Subjected to peer review and publication. Known or potential error rate and standards. Generally accepted by a relevant scientific community.

Relevance- "a brick is not a wall"

Why is something more prejudicial than probative? 403: assumes the evidence is relevant, you have to get past 401 and 402 first. The concerns must *substantially* outweigh the probative value. Fair v. unfair prejudice.

Something because character evidence because of what it is offered to show. Whether a court might rule something is **habit** or not depends on the level of prejudice sometimes

404(b) list isn't exceptions. Absence of mistake is simply *not* character evidence. The true exceptions are defame., entrap. (character might not *always* be at issue,). **Mercy rule** (my propensity to follow the law) is a true exception). Some courts allow char in quasi-criminal civils

Break apart pieces of evidence, don't just consider as a group

Evidence of a past false accusation of sex assault is *not* evidence of past behavior since it didn't happen, no rape shield. But collateral? But if it was a sex act that did happen, and the act was falsely called rape, then it does get rape shield even if it was consensual. Const. might trump 412

Specialized relevancy rules – partly a 403 rationale, partly broader public policy. Even if you pass the specialize rule, must still survive 403 balancing.

Crimen falsi: W / crim D must take stand

When char is in issue, it's in issue!

Self-defense, inclined to let in

Inferences from **flight** – courts skeptical, are you charged w other crimes?

from D's behavior to flight – **need strong evidence or indp corroboration**; flight to consciousness of guilt; to consciousness of guilt of charged crime; to actual guilt of charged crime

Juries over-value flight. absence of flight not sufficiently probative, but sneak in gently.

Reliability - *Rank hearsay*

What is it offered to prove *and* what can it come in for?

Hearsay must be statement, must be intentional to be statement. **See pg 354.**

"I am a grapefruit" is really: I think I am a grapefruit: is indirect assertion, is hearsay definitionally, why we have present state of mind

Analyze multiple ways to get it in, which hearsay fits, which doesn't, and why

More let in from children (tender years) with doctors

No bootstrapping! 801(d)(2) last sentence

Psychological underpinnings for why this exception is allowed

End

Always consider the jury

Problem with striking evidence once jury hears it is like the old country expression: "once the fish gets in the milk, it's hard to get the flavor out" – make objection before made

Closing argument

"Not by appearance shall he judge, nor by hearsay shall he decide. But he shall judge the poor with justice, and decide aright for the land's afflicted." Isaiah 11:3

Substantively: oath in the past & some cross

Rule	Topic	Availability conditions	Condition of statement
613	Past inconsistent statement offered to impeach – not for truth, gets limiting instruction	Dec must have testified	Good faith believe W made statement
801(d)(1)(A)	Past inconsistent statements offered substantively (not hearsay)	Must testify at trial and be subject to cross concerning the statement	Past statement was inconsistent and was given under oath at a "proceeding" or deposition
801(d)(1)(B)	Past consistent statements (not h)	Must testify at trial and be subject to cross concerning the statement	Statement is consistent, offered to rebut recent fabrication or improper motive, and *timing*
801(d)(1)(C)	Statement of Identification (not h)	Same	Identifies a person and was made after decl. perceived that person
804(b)(1)	Past testimony – hearsay exception	Must be unavailable	Statement was testimony under oath at a proceeding or deposition and subject to cross by party offered against with same motive
Insufficient memory			
612	Refreshing witness' memory	W on stand, memory exhausted	None, but if writing is used, 612 has rules
803*5)	Past recollection recorded	Must be on stand, must have insufficient rec	Record was made or adopted when witnesses memory was fresh and reflected correctly

For Con Law, I created my own annotated Constitution, which was super helpful for me. For any class that was driven by cases, such as Con Law and Election
Law, I created a list of cases with three- to five-word descriptions to jog my memory.
I am terrible at remembering case names, so this really helped. The point here is to
create short, simple, usable items that fit your particular needs for an exam. If you
remember case names better than I do, you will not need a crib sheet of cases. You
may not have time to flip through a 50-page outline to find the points you need, so
create smaller, more accessible tools (but still bring the 50-page outline just in case).

Use those tools when practicing for the exam and use your exam practice to
create and refine the tools. If you put together a road map for answering questions,
then use it to answer practice questions from commercial supplements. Look at the
sample answers in the exam and see if you left something out that you should have
included in your answer. If you did, then refine and add it to your model road map.
Finally, go through your custom open-book aids and see if there is anything you can
delete or get rid of. If you know some point so well that there is no risk of forgetting
it, then delete it to reduce the volume of junk your eyes have to pass over in taking
the exam.

Take-Home Exams

Take-home exams are more common at some law schools than others. At some
schools, students may graduate without ever experiencing a take-home exam. At
others, they might have a couple of take-home exams per semester. Take-home
exams present different challenges from in-class ones, and your strategy should
be adjusted accordingly.

Types and Styles of Take-Home Exams

The "traditional" take-home exam is designed to give students flexible scheduling. You pick up the exam when you want to—in a time that fits in your schedule
during the exam period—and return it within some set period of time, like 24
hours. Some exams may have a set time for you to pick the exam up; others
may have longer periods of time before you return it, like 48 hours or even a
week. Because of the extra time, such exams often include a word limit. Do not
play with the word limit.

I took an exam at Michigan that was a four-hour take-home exam that could be
picked up at any time during the exam period. A four-hour period for a take-home

exam that would have been a three-hour exam if taken in class didn't really provide enough time to take it home—most students took it in the library. The practical effect of that exam was really that we got to take it at the time that worked best for us. Although the style of take-home exams varies, the key features are limited but always include more time than a normal exam and freedom to move about or take the exam home with you.

The extra time and freedom does not make the exam easier. Remember, you are in law school and are graded on a curve. If the exam is easier for you, it is easier for everyone else, too. And if everyone gets the right answer, you need to be even more right to get a good grade. If, however, you have a solid strategy specific to take-home exams, you can use the unique format to your advantage.

Scheduling the Take-Home Exam

If you have a choice on when to take the exam, this can be one of your most important decisions. You have to know yourself to make a wise choice. In terms of the time of day to work on the exam, I am sure you already know whether you are a morning person or a night owl. Picking the *day* for the exam, though, can be more difficult. Assume that you have a two-week exam period with exams on the days in bold:

Monday	**Tuesday**	Wednesday	**Thursday**	Friday
Monday	Tuesday	Wednesday	Thursday	**Friday**

Possibly the most obvious time to squeeze in a take-home exam is on that last Thursday. It gives you the most time to study for the exam. Of course, that also gives you less time between exams—you will have one on Thursday and one on Friday. Pushing a take-home exam back to the end of the exam period also creates problems. What happens if all of your friends are done with their exams on Wednesday and are at the bar celebrating? You might want to join them, or get antsy. You can burn out and lose focus. You might not study well, or you might choose to take the exam earlier than you had planned just to get it over with.

Pick a time that works for you and that you know you can stick with, and then stick with it. Do not give in to pressure from others or from yourself to deviate from the plan and take the exam early. Generally, it is a good idea to give yourself a healthy amount of time between exams to study and switch mental gears. Unless you have a weeklong take-home exam, you should avoid taking other exams during the take-home exam period. Other types of planning depend on the type of take-home exam you face.

Planning for the Take-Home Exam

Once you've scheduled the exam, one of the key questions is where to take it. If the exam is short, such as two to four hours, plan on taking it at school, in the library or some equivalent place. Taking the exam on campus eliminates travel time and reduces complications. It probably provides multiple printer choices (assuming you turn in a printed copy). But as with all advice in this book, you have to make it work for you. Libraries tend to be very crowded during exams, and if your school has a lot of take-home exams, this can only add to the chaos. In other words, use the library unless there is a better option. It is also a good idea to play your logistics. Know ahead of time where you have to turn the exam in and if that place has limited hours. Figure out where to print the exam and have a backup plan. Know where to plug in your computer. Have food plans. If you are going to take the exam in the library, what will you do with your stuff when you go to the bathroom?

If the take-home exam period is 24 hours, stick to your normal cycle of eat, sleep, and exercise. The exam process is primarily about mental focus and analysis, so keep your brain functioning well. If the take-home exam is open-book, then consult the advice set out in this chapter's open-book section.

Use the Time

Your professor gave you 4 hours or 24 hours for a reason. Use that time, if only because others might. Having more time to work on an exam can mean that the expectations are higher or the curve is harder. Once your analysis is sound, use the remaining time to format the exam, proofread it, and fix your spelling. Budget some time for a final proofread of the exam. If you have plenty of time, step away from your work for a while. Go for a little a walk to clear your head and look at the paper with fresh eyes. Use the writing process you would apply to an essay or paper when given enough time to actually do so.

No Cheating!

Do not even fudge the rules. If your professor tells you not to use Westlaw, then do not use LexisNexis either. This advice applies to all exams and every aspect of law school. But the temptation is much greater with take-home exams because no one is around to see you take the exam and students may end up taking the exam at different times. Do not talk about the exam with other students who have not taken it yet. The consequences of breaking these rules can be huge. If you cheat, assist someone else in cheating, or fail to report someone else for cheating, you could be denied admission to the bar even if your school does not kick you out. Many people think lawyers are scum, but they self-regulate very energetically, perhaps in part because of that scummy reputation.

Pass/Fail Exams

Not every law school features pass/fail exams. Some schools permit students to elect to take a class pass/fail before, during, or even after a semester. This presents strategic considerations both in making the election and in how to prepare for it.

Consider what you need to do to pass the class, how it will look to take the class pass/fail (will the patent attorney interviewing you ask why you pass/failed patent law?), and what you hope to accomplish by taking it pass/fail. The University of Michigan permits students to take multiple classes pass/fail. I made the election in three of them.

Transnational Law—basically just international law—is a required course at Michigan. I was not particularly interested in the topic and made the choice to take it pass/fail at the start of the semester so that I could focus on other graded classes and try to ace those. From the very start of the semester I put in just enough work to pass. I did not plan on getting much out of Transnational Law and simply needed to pass the required class.

The next semester I took Secured Transactions pass/fail. The class was taught by famous professor J.J. White. I wanted to learn a lot about the subject, but I was mostly interested in taking a class with J.J. White. Due to his semiretired status, the class was taught in an intense two-and-a-half-week period, and I was required to choose pass/fail status early on (at the time, Michigan allowed students to choose pass/fail up until they took the exam). I found the subject matter very difficult and chose pass/fail early on to protect my GPA. Shortly after the midterm (given in the second week of the class), the material clicked, and I slightly regretted the pass/fail choice. I still made an effort to learn the material, though, and was thrilled to have a class with J.J. White.

That semester I also took another class in a subject I was very interested in. I had high hopes for the class and thought I would have a chance do very well. It became abundantly clear to me in the first week, though, that the long-tenured professor had no interest in teaching the subject matter at all. This professor spent the entire hour ranting about policy issues. In fairness, some of those issues did relate to the subject matter, but we were not learning the substantive law as expected in the class. This was my last semester. I wanted to preserve my GPA, but my senioritis kept me from switching to a different class—this one fit so well into my schedule. I took it pass/fail, as did almost everyone in the class. I showed up and completely tuned out. Needless to say, it is not a good idea to tell your professor in this kind of situation why you took the class pass/fail. I regret that I had to take it pass/fail, but I did it defensively and used the extra time to work on other projects. Making the decision to give up on the class early on allowed me to reallocate that time and gave me my highest GPA ever in that last semester.

Another friend chose to take a class pass/fail at the last possible minute. He studied hard all semester, gunning for a good grade. But as exam day drew closer he grew concerned and felt he would not do well. To me, it seemed like a lot of wasted effort over the course of a semester to elect to take the class pass/fail at the last minute. But he rightly saw that the effort would be even more wasted if he dinged his GPA. Ideally, if you choose to take a class pass/fail, you will study just enough to pass the class and learn the basics of the material. Failing it would not be fun. But limiting your studying to just what's needed can give you a comfortable margin to focus on excelling in other classes.

Key Points

- Take steps to improve your skills at multiple-choice questions.
- Make a conscious effort to manage your time during exams.
- Answering questions to which you immediately know the answer first, then completing essays, and finally returning to the multiple-choice questions you need to think about is often a helpful strategy for better ensuring you complete your exam in time.
- Prepare for multiple-choice questions by answering multiple-choice practice questions in books and supplements and flagging why you got an answer wrong.
- Policy questions tend to be very subjective and difficult to prepare for. Understand the policy, the "why" behind the law, and take notes on your professor's policy analysis.

- If you have trouble remembering case names, creating a crib sheet of the cases with three to five words to jog your memory can be very helpful for an open-book exam, as is a condensed version of your larger course outline.
- Be calculating and careful in choosing the time and location in which to complete a take-home exam.
- Do not cheat! Cheating, whether you cheat or help someone cheat, can affect your entry into the bar even if your school does not kick you out.
- Be strategic in your approach to taking a class pass/fail.

Chapter 7

Legal Research and Writing Classes: Research and Writing, and What to Expect in Research and Writing Classes

LEARNING THE ART OF LEGAL WRITING IS ARGUABLY THE MOST IMPORTANT PART of law school. Your legal writing classes are supposed to teach you an actual skill, unlike most of your classes, and almost every single job you can do with a law degree requires some exercise of writing skills. Students with excellent legal writing grades but less-than-stellar overall GPAs sometimes list a separate legal writing GPA on their resume. Some students naturally develop these skills; others find the process difficult and face repeated frustrations in class.

Legal writing is a distinct type of writing, and some who fancy themselves good writers—even those with English or journalism backgrounds—could find themselves receiving surprisingly low marks in class. Two of legal writing's key features—supporting just about every assertion with some kind of authority and persuasively weaving in cases in the common law style—do not come naturally to all.

This style of writing is different from writing for undergraduate English classes in several ways. It requires a high degree of precision in language use. Legal standards and concepts turn on small details that have to be captured accurately in writing. Structure is also more important and more formal, so much that elegant legal writing actually looks simple at first glance. The audience is almost always more demanding, as your legal writing professors were all trained in this specific art and will demand that you follow the same rules and conventions they do. Legal writing must be done a certain way, and there is often little room for variation.

Legal writing classes also provide one of the experiences that varies most between law schools. While your substantive 1L classes, such as Contracts and Civil Procedure, will generally be taught with the same content and style as at other law schools, the legal writing curriculum can differ sharply. The number of credits, workload, and whether a class is graded or ungraded vary. The type of instructor varies, too, from tenured legal writing professors to untenured legal writing faculty, fellows, and teaching assistants.

The standard model, however, is a two-semester class, with the first semester covering writing a closed memo (using only a limited set of cases provided by the instructor) and then an open memo (performing actual legal research). The second semester class, sometimes given a different name such as Moot Court, covers writing something persuasive, such as an appellate or summary judgment brief, and then arguing it. The level of difficulty will be determined by the topics your professor selects, the expectations he or she has, and the class's grading structure.

These classes often carry fewer credits than the substantive classes but can be a tremendous time drain. Striking the right balance in allocating time to legal writing and to substantive classes can be quite difficult, especially with a demanding, graded class. Try not to put in so much time that your other classes suffer, but do not deprioritize legal writing to the point that you do poorly or fail to learn the necessary skills. The best way to strike the right balance is to take advantage of the timing differences between the classes. You can write your brief or memo early, but you cannot do an exam early. If you practice good time-management and complete your legal writing projects in the middle of the semester, or at least before the deadline, you will have the last stretch to dedicate entirely to exam preparation. Taking advantage of the timeline and all available resources can help you to excel in legal writing without putting your other grades at risk.

While this chapter is not enough to make you a great legal writer, it should help you excel in legal writing classes. There are many books dedicated to legal writing, and the limited coverage here is not meant to be read in place of those. Typically, you will be assigned one of those books. Books like *Plain English for Lawyers*, by Richard Wydick, or *Legal Writing in Plain English*, by Bryan Garner, can be very helpful.

If you do not want to pay for a book or feel you do not have time to read something that long, you can find quite a bit of help for free in law journals. For example, you could punch one of these citations into Westlaw after you learn how to use it: Richard C. Wydick, *True Confessions of a Diddle-Diddle Dumb-Head*, 11 Scribes J. Legal Writing 57 (2007), or Bryan Garner, *Cultivate the Right Demeanor for Effective Legal Writing*, 89-FEB Mich. B.J. 46 (2010). If you are looking for advice on performing oral arguments in class, take a look at James D. Dimitri, *Stepping Up to the Podium With Confidence: A Primer for Law Students on Preparing and Delivery an Apellate Oral Argument*, 38 Stetson L. Rev. 75 (2008) or Michael S. Kanne, *10 Tips for Improving Your Oral Argument*, 17 No. 4 PRACLIT 17 (2006).

With those qualifiers, I will briefly offer some tips on developing the skills you need for legal research and writing, how to avoid some of the common mistakes that law students make, and how to write briefs and memos that deserve high grades.

Developing Legal Research and Writing Skills

Once you develop legal research and writing skills, you can apply them to any assignment. Start by seriously paying attention in your legal writing class and take notes on the research and writing topics covered, even if they seem obvious or trivial. Some students make the mistake of thinking that they already understand legal writing because they are good writers or that the research tasks are simple, until they get the harder assignments dumped on them later in the semester. Do not fall into that trap, and instead give your professor's instruction the respect it deserves.

Take advantage of everything your professor will do for you. If he or she agrees to look over a draft and give you feedback on it if you turn it in early, do it. If he or she is willing to meet with you to discuss your paper after it was turned in (rather than merely returning it with red pen marks), do it, and come prepared with questions. Do not just accept the red pen marks; ask why they are there and try to understand. Make a personal list of things you screw up on, try to fix them, and then check your next draft or assignment against that list. Constantly improve your writing. Realize that writing is a process that requires constant improvement—not just on a given assignment, but on your overall style and abilities.

It is also important to develop basic *Bluebook* (or *ALWD Citation Manual*, if your professor uses that) and citation skills—knowing the proper way to format the cases, statutes, and other authorities you use throughout your writing assignment. If your professor gives you a cheat sheet or some instruction on the topic, pay serious attention to it. Once you learn how to cite authorities, it seems like a really easy thing, but some students initially struggle with the citation formats. In particular, make sure you know how to use short cites.

If you are struggling, pay attention to how the citations are formatted in the cases you read or in sample briefs and memos. If something is particularly tricky, you can open the source in Westlaw or LexisNexis and run a KeyCite or Shepard's report to get an idea of how the source is cited in other cases. You should become familiar with your *Bluebook*, though, so that you know how to look up the right format when you need to.

Because the exact methods of legal research—the interface and search tools of the legal databases—are likely to change, I am not going to provide specific advice on how to use Westlaw or LexisNexis. Becoming proficient at finding what you need in these amazing legal databases must be one of your top priorities. While you will undoubtedly end up favoring one service over another, it is best to establish a minimum proficiency in both services because future employers might have only one or the other.

Your basic research goal is to learn the governing law and find the relevant cases. In most legal writing class assignments, you will be applying case law, even if there is an underlying statute or rule that this case law interprets. There will usually be a particularly important case or set of cases (the leading case) and a series of cases applying it. I often picture it as a tree, with the leading case that sets out the doctrine or the test you need as the trunk and all the cases applying the leading case and quibbling over whether a certain fact pattern meets the test as the branches that come out from this trunk.

With this mental image, I start a case-law search using the best search terms I can come up with (and refining my search as I read more cases and get a better understanding of what I am looking for). If I find a case covering my topic, it will probably either cite the trunk case or a case that is closer to the trunk. I look for the case that others cite and look to—if they call the four-factor test "the *Miller* test," I look for the case named *Miller*. Once I am on the trunk, I can use Westlaw's KeyCite or LexisNexis's Shepard's to find all the branches and look for the ones that are most on-point, which means most like the situation faced in a writing assignment, and most recent.

While I often start with a case-law search in my attempt to find the leading cases, there are several other ways to begin researching. Some start by looking for a treatise or a secondary source (something like *American Law Reports* or *Moore's Federal*

Practice). Not only will a source like this explain the law in general terms, it will cite the leading cases in either its text or footnotes. Others find the statute or rule involved, if there is one, and look at the annotations to the statute for the cases they need. A great researcher knows how to use all these tools and can pick the one best suited for a particular assignment. The only way you are going to learn the different research methods is through practice and training.

Your legal writing instructor will probably spend some time showing you how to research, or he or she might bring in the training representatives from Westlaw and LexisNexis. As with all of your classes, pay attention, follow along, and take notes. If your professor is old-school or sees the value in using print resources, he or she might assign you to do certain research tasks with the books in the library. The print resources can give you a context for electronic resources. Knowing that "23 F.3d 233" means that you need to find volume 23 (the book with "23" on the front of it) in the *Federal Reporter* series and go to page 233 of that book, may help you understand what all the citations you are typing into Westlaw really mean. While you should do as you are told, make sure you learn how to use the electronic databases, as these are much more efficient for most of what you are doing.

The Westlaw and LexisNexis training reps will probably conduct training seminars at your school outside of class throughout the year (usually with free pizza if the seminars are held during the lunch hour). These are excellent opportunities, and you should try to attend as many as you can. Keep your eyes open for online postings or flyers on your school bulletin boards that tell you when the seminars are held. An hour of training can save you several hours of frustration later. If you are struggling with the research tools, you can also talk to the Westlaw or LexisNexis student representatives or your law librarians. But do not let the legal databases blind you to other sources—sometimes a simple Google search will tell you what you need to know on a topic.

Knowing how to find things can also help you find tools to build up your legal writing skills. For some students, it can be hard to develop legal writing skills without ever having encountered legal writing. If your professor's instruction is not getting through to you, or if you were disappointed in the grade on your first project, this advice might be particularly relevant. In general, reading is a good way to gain knowledge about writing, and you can use this principle to help you with class by finding good legal writing to look over.

Your assigned textbook may have sample memos and briefs, and this should be your starting point. Sometimes, though, it can be helpful to look at more than one sample to see what they all have in common. You can find great legal memos on the Web site of the Office of Legal Counsel (*http://www.justice.gov/olc/*), a part of the attorney general's office that prepares formal legal memos for the president. You can find briefs on Westlaw or LexisNexis. Westlaw's ALLBRIEFS database makes this easy, and you can also click the link on many of the cases you read on Westlaw to find the briefs for that case. Scanning through a few briefs gives you an idea of how to format your own and can help you with your writing.

Looking over good examples of legal writing can help you pick up some of the finer style points. For example, legal writers generally avoid using contractions (e.g., they say "cannot" instead of "can't," "it is" instead of "it's"). We use the serial comma ("item 1, item 2, and item 3" rather than "item 1, item 2 and item 3)" because it prevents ambiguity when dealing with complicated lists. And we use the full range of punctuation marks: We use a colon when leading off into a complex list; we use a semicolon when separating complete sentences or in lists that are otherwise too complicated (such as a list of the elements of a tort or legal test where each element itself has commas within it); and we use a dash (—) for emphasis on a pause stronger than that conveyed by a comma.

Writing for Your Legal Writing Class

I cannot stress how valuable it is to get your legal writing assignments done early in the semester rather than waiting until the end, and to make an effort to work with your professor and take advantage of any resources he or she might offer. If your professor provides a grading rubric, you should consult it as you go along to ensure you put an appropriate amount of effort into less-obvious areas (such as citation formatting) that might be worth a lot of points.

Your writing assignments will likely consist of memos at firsts and briefs later. In both assignments you undertake a very similar research and writing exercise. You want to lay out the facts of your case (preferably chronologically) and apply the law. Arguments should usually be ordered from strongest to weakest. If you have a question on jurisdiction (whether the court can properly hear the case) or some other procedural issue that would preclude ruling on the merits, you should usually address this first. While this analysis will be research-driven, do not ignore obvious policy arguments or effects that should be discussed—for example, how ruling that Tasers constitute deadly force might make police more likely to use firearms to shoot armed suspects.

Whether to write your facts first or your argument or analysis is a matter of taste. Some write the facts first to get the project moving and set up the overall project the right way. Others write the facts second to make sure that only facts necessary to the legal reasoning that follows are included. In both memos and briefs you should wait to write the summary until you have finished the argument or analysis.

The difference between memos and briefs is primarily that memos are more balanced. Even so, the reader wants to know the strengths and weaknesses of arguments, but they are simply presented in a balanced rather than persuasive style. Both kinds of assignments require you to avoid common mistakes and produce good writing.

Tips on Avoiding Common Mistakes

Before you get to the level of great legal writing, you have to avoid the common mistakes. Some students instinctively avoid these pitfalls and can focus on the finer nuances of legal writing right away. Others struggle with issues such as accuracy of language, leaving out the "because," not understanding how to use cases, and poor timing.

Legal writing requires a high degree of precision. If the district court dismissed the case, do not use the language and rules associated with *summary judgment*. If the court granted summary judgment, do not say the case was dismissed. Match the right words to the right legal terms, rules, and standards.

Many students can state the standard and that their facts meet the standard, but have trouble explaining why—they leave out the "because." After stating the factors that make up a legal test and the facts, you need to explain why you meet that standard. That you meet the test may seem too obvious to explain or intuitive, but assume the reader does not know the facts or the law the way you do. Keep in mind that you are explaining the correct outcome to a person who does not know what you know.

As the reader does not share the expertise you built up doing research, you have to explain more about certain cases. Let me give you a quick example. Suppose that in a brief for a criminal case, you have established that a defendant needs to establish his relationship to a hotel room before being able to challenge an unconstitutional search of that room. In cases where the defendant uses a pseudonym to obtain the room, the court asks whether the defendant had the de facto or unofficial permission of the hotel owner to use a fake name—in other words, whether the owner was okay with defendant Smith using a fake name to get the room.

In the paragraph where you set out the controlling law, you can do so by citing or quoting the cases without wading into the details of the cases—you can simply extract the law you need and set it out as a controlling standard. Certain cases, though, in which the facts are analogous or need to be distinguished, need to be treated in more detail. Here is how you might use cases in the analysis portion of a brief (though note that these cases are hypothetical):

> In *Miller*, the defendant used an "obviously false identification" to register for the hotel room. *United States v. Miller*, 253 F.2d 237, 239 (6th Cir. 1976). The hotel clerk accepted a cash payment before making a copy of Miller's novelty identification card, which listed the holder's name as John Doe, the state as Californication, "and the sex as 'please.'" *Id.* at 239-40. Miller also offered evidence that the hotel had a pattern of questionable registrations and that the owner accepted this conduct by the clerks. *Id.* at 240. Accordingly, the court found "that the absurdity of Miller's identification and the hotel's pattern of accepting cash payments without proper (or sometimes any) ID demonstrated that Miller rented the room with the de facto permission of the motel owner." *Id.*
>
> Similarly, Smith paid cash, offered to pay additional $20 if he did not have to show identification, and then wrote "Don Juan" as his name on the registration card when the motel owner accepted the extra payment. By allowing Smith to pay extra to avoid disclosing his real identity and accepting a humorous name on the registration, this motel owner gave Smith de facto, if not explicit, permission to rent the room under a false name.
>
> While *United States v. Rac*, 237, F.3d 253, 257 (6th Cir. 1942) required a pattern of accepting false registrations to establish de facto permission, the defendant in that case rented the room from a clerk, rather than directly from the owner, necessitating some additional proof of the owner's acquiescence to this type of transaction. *See id.* at 254. As Smith received permission to register under a false identity directly from the owner, he need not show a pattern of false registrations to establish the owner's permission.

Because I decided that *Miller* was my most important case, I gave the case a full treatment. I detailed its facts, quoted its relevant holding, and then tried to show how the facts in my case lined up. A reader should be able to see from the similarity between your case and the case you are relying on that the outcome ought to be the same. Parallelism can help to draw the reader's attention to it. In explaining the *Miller* case, I put the details in the order of cash, bogus ID, and information about the owner. In relating *Smith's* facts, I mentioned that the defendant paid in cash, used a bogus ID, and dealt directly with the owner. This can be done much more eloquently, but I hope this example helps to show how you can treat a case and show its relationship to yours.

Not every case requires a full treatment. Sometimes you simply need to distinguish the case in a sentence or two, as I tried to above after anticipating the counter-argument about needing to show a pattern. If you can persuasively distinguish a case with a few words, then do not waste time by giving it a full treatment.

One final mistake some students make is not putting enough time into their writing project, timing it poorly (waiting until the last minute), or simply being lazy. If you know from the start that your paper will need editing, then you know you need to complete it with enough time before the deadline to allow for editing.

Tips on Editing

You should plan to set aside time for editing. It is important to hand in a polished draft rather than a rough draft. Even if your class has you turn in a first draft of your assignment to your professor and get his or her feedback before you turn in a final version, plan on editing that first draft. The better the paper you give to your professor to get feedback on, the better the feedback will be and the closer you will get to the great final grade you want.

Give yourself time to do multiple edits over multiple days—set your paper aside after making a round of edits and look at it the next day with fresh eyes. Doing this means that you will have to finish the rough draft earlier, but it is worth it. Your editing should generate cuts in the length of your first draft. In legal writing, longer is not necessary better.

Smaller briefs are usually better in actual legal practice, and this is still somewhat true for class—that your page limit is twenty pages is not necessarily a reason to use all twenty pages, although this can be a hard line to draw when you want to avoid disappointing a professor's expectations on length. But in all cases, do not write extra pages just to add to the length (as you might have done in college) and eliminate unnecessary words.

Wordiness is a real problem in the legal profession. Many come into law school knowing how to write and speak English like a human being and within a few weeks start using unnecessary words and legalese, erroneously assuming that this makes them sound smarter. Read your draft, preferably out loud, and look for unnecessary words. Say the defendant "moved" instead of "filed a motion" or the police "assumed" instead of "made an assumption." And you almost never need to say "the fact that." Poor legal writing often uses a lot of long sentences. Some legal concepts are complex and really do require compound sentences. But short sentences add punch. Comb through your legal writing to see if your sentences are unnecessarily long and consider breaking up a few for the reader's benefit. While you are cutting words in the editing process, you might find places to add words to make transitions. Good writing connects sentences and paragraphs by having one end with something similar to the start of the next. Nice transitions make your work much more readable and can make the flow more logical.

Tips on Carefully Using the Special Tools of the Trade

One of the defining features of legal writing is the use of authority or citations to the record (the affidavits, transcripts, or documents that the facts come from) to back up points. Make sure your citations to cases and the record are accurate, not just formatted correctly. If your quote is not right or you attribute it to the wrong page, your professor might notice, especially since your classmates might all be using the same quotes. But beyond the basics of using cases discussed above, you should understand a few special ways that authority is presented.

When used in moderation, parentheticals are a great tool of the legal writer. This is where you put a quote after a citation: *Answers in Genesis of Ky., Inc. v. Creation Ministries Int'l, Ltd.*, 556 F.3d 459, 465 (6th Cir. 2009) ("federal courts have a duty to consider their subject matter jurisdiction in regard to every case and may raise the issue *sua sponte*"). Parentheticals need not include full quotes; some include a short statement like "(defendant who used novelty ID, paid clerk in cash, and established pattern of conduct had de facto permission)" and others include an even shorter explanation like "(trademark case)." You do not need a parenthetical after every case you cite, and too many can bog down your writing.

It is best to use a quote parenthetical when it follows a statement in which you paraphrased the court's holding or made a conclusion of your own that the quote eloquently backs up, and to use a paraphrased parenthetical (in which you summarize the holding) when you need to show the reader how the holding or facts of that case line up with your case or provide some context, such as that you are quoting a trademark case in support of something related to your argument about copyright law.

Parentheticals are often placed after citations that involve the signals *see, see also, but see, compare, contra, accord, c.f,* and so on. The *Bluebook* sets out its official explanation for using these signals in Rule 1.2; the *ALWD Citation Manual* sets it out in Rule 44. Take a moment to read the rule that applies to your class. This is an easy way to get points. The two most common signals you will need to know are *see* and *see, e.g.*

If the case or authority you are citing *directly* supports the sentence you put it after, you do not need to use the signal *see.* This means that using *see* after a quotation or after every sentence is not right. Some attorneys like to put *see* in because they think it looks cool. Your legal writing professor probably knows the rule and will not think it looks cool if used inappropriately. Use *see* when the case supports the proposition in the sentence before it but not directly—when an inference is needed. For example, if you say that the existence of probable cause is a fact-intense inquiry, and the court case does not use that language but talks about how the court needs to review all relevant facts and the opinion spends pages dealing with facts, you might use *see.* When you use *see,* you should consider whether a parenthetical is necessary for the reader to grasp the inference. In my example, you would look to the case and see whether a reader checking your citation would realize that the case supports your proposition. If not, you might use a parenthetical like "performing detailed review of facts."

The other signal you will likely use often is *see, e.g.* Technically, this is the combination of two signals—the rules treat *see* and *e.g.* as separate signals. When combined together they stand for the proposition that the cited case or cases support your proposition *and* that there are other cases not cited because they are too numerous to cite or because it simply would not be helpful to cite them all. Sometimes it is appropriate to use *see, e.g.* with only one case after it. You might have a sentence claiming that it is a well-established rule that something or other is the law. Here, a *see, e.g.* signal tells the reader that a lot of cases say what this one says, but you really only need to cite this one since it is such a well-established rule. Commonly, though, you will *see, e.g.,* before a string cite, indicating that you have other cases that support this same proposition but are not included. You can only use the *e.g.* if there actually are other cases that could be used.

When using a string cite—a series of cases listed in a row used to support a point—you will almost always want to use parentheticals after the cases, although the exact choice of quotes, paraphrasing, or a simple "(same)" to tell the reader that the second case reaches the same conclusion as the first, will vary based on what you are using the string cite for.

String cites are a very valuable tool in legal writing that can also bog down readers and look ugly on the page. Just because you have a bunch of cases that say the same thing or agree on the legal conclusion does not mean that you have to cite them all. String cites work well when you need to show responses from different jurisdictions, such as when you are saying that every circuit that has considered the issue agrees with you or claiming that there is a circuit split, and then listing the cases with appropriate parentheticals. You might also use a string cite to show different fact permutations that reach the same conclusion, using parentheticals to show the facts. Of course there are other times when string cites are appropriate, but before using a string cite, ask yourself why exactly you want to use the string cite and consider whether an alternative—perhaps not using some of the citations or breaking up the string cite to have a sentence supported by each citation—works better.

Similar considerations should go into using footnotes. Before using a footnote, ask yourself whether you could put the footnote text in the main document and whether you need the text at all. To the extent possible, you should try to avoid using footnotes in briefs and memos. There is no rule against footnotes, though, and they are appropriate in some circumstances. One of the most frequent uses I have seen is to explain why something is not being addressed substantively in the text. If there is an eight-factor legal test and you are only arguing six factors because two are uncontested, it might make sense to drop a footnote that tells the reader that the other two factors are undisputed. If you are writing an appellate brief and your fact section says the plaintiff raised three claims below, but only two are being argued on appeal, you might drop a footnote someplace convenient (perhaps at the start of your argument section) to explicitly state that only two of the three claims are raised on appeal and that the remaining claim is waived.

Be just as careful with block quotes. The *Bluebook* requires that quotations of fifty words or more be placed in block quotes—single-spaced and indented on both sides. Most readers hate reading block quotes, and our eyes often want to simply skip over them. Block quotes can be a nice way of presenting certain information, such as the factors of some multifactor legal test, but consider the alternatives before using one.

Tips on the Standard of Review

The standard of review is a very important section in both briefs and memos. For a trial court, the standard has to do with the relief sought and when that relief is sought. This means that a for a trial court, the rule under which you are making a motion will likely govern whether you are entitled to relief. On appeal, the standard of review depends on what lower court (or agency) ruling is being appealed and on what grounds.

Getting the standard of review right is the best way to start your legal analysis. The language of the standard of review should influence the way you write the remaining sections. This is important in memos, but even more so in persuasive briefs. If you are dealing with an appellate case, you must identify the error that the district court made that justifies reversal in light of the standard of review you set out.

When writing a brief, research the standard of review carefully to find the right quotes to frame that standard the right way. If you can, treat the standard of review as a part of your argument, and work it in throughout your arguments. There are three basic standards of appellate review: de novo (usually for legal determinations), clearly erroneous (usually for factual determinations), and abuse of discretion (usually for judgment calls).

"De novo" is a type of fresh review in which the appellate court gives no deference to the lower court's ruling. "Clearly erroneous" gives more deference to the trial judge. A factual determination is "clearly erroneous" when although there is evidence to support it, the reviewing court on the entire evidence is left with the definite and firm conviction that a mistake has been committed." *United States v. Mabry*, 518 F.3d 442, 449 (6th Cir. 2008). If you are trying to overturn a ruling under this standard, you must push hard to show that the judge had the facts wrong—not that it was a toss-up. If you are trying to uphold the ruling, you can stand on the standard and show that, even if there is some confusion as to what is going on, the appellate tribunal cannot have a firm conviction that the district court was mistaken.

"Abuse of discretion" is even more deferential. "A district court abuses its discretion if it bases its rulings on an erroneous view of the law or a clearly erroneous assessment of the evidence." *Ky. Speedway, LLC v. Nat'l Assoc. of Stock Car Auto Racing, Inc.*, 588 F.3d 908, 915 (6th Cir. 2009) (quotation marks and citation omitted). If you are arguing that the district court abused its discretion, you might seize on the language about an erroneous view of the law and show that the court relied on a bad interpretation of law to make the challenged ruling.

Whatever standard you face, figure it out right away so you can frame your argument or analysis properly.

Special Considerations in Briefs

In the practice of law, the written brief is much more important than the oral argument, if oral argument is even held. Likewise, in your 1L classes, the brief is a much bigger part of your grade than oral argument and accordingly deserves more of your time. The nature of brief-writing requires some special attention to certain details and formatting requirements.

Argumentative writing can tempt some to use extreme descriptive words. Never call your opponent's arguments ridiculous or silly. Keep your arguments focused on the law rather than making them personal. If the opposing argument is meritless or unsupported by precedent, say so, but do not make those claims unless you can back them up. In a similar vein, avoid all distortions of the law or the facts—once you lose credibility with the reader, you cannot get it back. Make your argument within the rules, rather than breaking them.

Consulting the court rules for formatting is extremely important for most 1L classes and, to a lesser extent, the legal profession. Your brief must fit within page limits and include certain sections specified in the rules (or in your class assignment). If your professor provides a grading rubric for the brief, study it. If a significant percentage of your grade comes from sections other than your argument, such as the summary of the argument or statement of the issues, make sure you put in the time there to pick up the easy points.

The statement of the issues in a brief should be persuasive but short and should properly frame the issues for the rest of your brief. The statement should ideally include both law and facts and lead the reader to want to answer "yes." Not something like:

Should the trial court's grant of summary judgment be reversed?

But like:

Does a genuine issue of material fact exist as to the color of the stoplight at the time of the crash, when plaintiff testified it was red and defendant testified it was green?

Or:

Did the court abuse its discretion in awarding sole child custody to Mr. Jones without permitting the ten-year-old child, who was present in the courtroom, to express her preference for shared custody with Mrs. Smith?

Setting the right tone up front helps you to convince the reader later.

In the first sentence of your statement of the case or statement of the facts (depending on the rule), tell the court what your case is about and frame it in a way that helps you. You might actually say "This case is about" or you might phrase it more artfully, but a one-sentence summary at the very start of your brief is important to the reader and reminds you to stay on track.

When you write a statement of the facts, it is important to stay accurate and avoid arguing within the fact section. Generally, a chronological telling of the facts is best. Though you have to be fair, you should still tell a story—specifically, the story that benefits your client. Subtly present the client's story in a way that leads the reader to want your side to win before the reader even reaches the legal arguments. Do not ignore the fact section even in a case where the argument rests primarily on legal, rather than factual, issues.

The summary of your argument is essentially a quick argument without citations. It is okay to include a controlling case (like a Supreme Court case) or statute in this section, but you do not need the kind of case citation that you use in your argument. The topic sentences and concluding sentences from your argument section should give you the tools you need to write the summary.

The argument section is the meat of your brief and probably where the most points come from in your class. As mentioned earlier, you should use the standard order in legal writing, putting the strongest arguments first and the weakest last, unless you need to address something like jurisdiction. Your decision on which arguments to present also affects your persuasiveness. Strong arguments sound weaker if surrounded by weak arguments, and bad arguments cause you to lose credibility. Sometimes it is best to simply leave a weak argument out of the brief.

Section headings and subheadings are particularly important in briefs. Keep in mind that the memos you may have written and the court opinions you read for class are different, as they tend to use descriptive headings. You want argumentative headings in a brief. Each heading should summarize the argument to follow by touching on the relevant facts, the applicable law, and the conclusion your argument will reach. The headings also organize your thinking and transition to the argument that follows. Once you have put your brief together, look through your table of contents to see if your headings, read in a row, basically summarize your entire argument.

Your arguments should be research-driven, which means that it is very hard to start the writing process until you have done the necessary research. The basic format of an argumentative paragraph is the Contention, Rule, Analysis, Conclusion (CRAC) method, which you will hear about in class. This means that you state first a topic sentence, then the precedents that set out the rule, then how those precedents support your position, tying them into the facts of your case to show that they logically support your position. Try to make your result seem simple, easy, natural, and conservative. Doing so will convince the court, or your professor, to award you what you want.

What to Do If Things Go Wrong

If a bad grade on a legal writing assignment or for your first semester of Legal Writing catches you by surprise, there are steps you can take to turn it around. The first step is to swallow your pride and recognize that you need help with legal writing. Talk to your instructor to find out what you could do better. Take advantage of any tutoring your school offers and see if any of the student organizations (Black Students Alliance, Federalist Society, and so on) offer support or advice to their members.

Next, make an effort to read up on legal writing, either by studying your assigned book or by purchasing one of the other books described above, and then look over what you turned in and try to identify your weaknesses. If you struggled with memos, put extra effort into your briefs (assuming your class switches from memos to briefs) and study up on memos before starting to write the brief. Many brilliant attorneys have written about how to write effective briefs. You can access some of these through Westlaw, LexisNexis, or your school's library. *See, e.g.,* Stephen Dwyer et al., *How to Write, Edit, and Review Persuasive Briefs: Seven Guidelines from One Judge and Two Lawyers*, 31 Seattle U. L. Rev. 417 (2008); Brian Porto, *The Art of Appellate Brief Writing*, 29 Vt. B.J. 30 (2003). Finally, do not give up; you can get better.

Key Points

- Legal writing classes often involve fewer credits than the more substantive subject courses, but still can involve a tremendous amount of time and require striking a balance between writing and studying for other courses that have final exams.

- Completing your legal writing projects by the middle of the semester and before the deadline can allow you to dedicate the last half of the semester to exam preparation.

- Carefully note the research and writing topics covered by your professor in your legal writing course.

- Take advantage of anything your professor will do for you, such as looking over drafts, meeting with you to discuss your paper, etc. Turn in a polished copy for review to get the most constructive feedback on the content of the writing.

- Develop good citation skills and skills using Bluebook or AWLD, depending on professor preference.

- Become efficient and effective in the use of Westlaw and LexisNexis.

- Pay careful attention to any grading rubrics provided by your instructor.

- Order arguments from strongest to weakest.

- The statement of the issues in a brief should be persuasive, but short, and properly frame the issues for the rest of your brief.

- If you receive a poor mark on a legal writing assignment, accept and seek out help to improve your skills, approach, and methods. Continual work on improving your writing abilities can prevent the poor marks in the future.

Chapter 8

DECISIONS MADE AFTER THE FIRST YEAR

THE FIRST YEAR OF LAW SCHOOL IS A DIFFICULT, CRAZY EXPERIENCE that takes forever to get through but also goes by very quickly. When you come up for air after the first year is over, it is time to take a long hard look at some of your options. If you had great success in law school, this might include transferring to a higher-ranked law school. If you did poorly or are worried that the debt you are taking on is not justified by the career prospects, you might seriously consider leaving school. However you did during the first year, you should seriously think about your options rather than trudging along by default.

Whether to Stay in Law School

Law students have dropped out at the end of the first year (or at the end of the first semester, first week of class, or first day of class) for years. Only in recent years, though, has this actually been discussed more broadly and sometimes even praised. For example, a first-year student at a top 50 (but not top 14) school wrote to the popular legal tabloid AboveTheLaw.com in November 2010 asking whether he should drop out. His reasoning was simple: He was taking on $21,000 in debt per semester of law school, believed the job market for lawyers to be oversaturated, and thought that whatever job he landed after law school would not justify this massive debt. A poll of AboveTheLaw.com's readers—mostly cynical lawyers and law students—said he should drop out by a margin of 78 percent to 22 percent. Make the decision that is right for you.

Transferring Law Schools

If you go to the admissions section of a law school's Web site, they almost all tell you that they are looking at you holistically. They care about diversity or your life experience or other such important things. But by coincidence, members of a school's entering class—the one selected through a "holistic process"—seem to have pretty similar LSAT scores and GPAs every year. This is because schools report the incoming class's LSATs and undergrad GPAs to *U.S. News and World Report* as factors in the magazine's annual rankings. Transfer students, on the other hand, do not count toward a school's rankings. Some schools take advantage of this to bring in additional students after their first year, either because the students are very promising or the school could use a few more tuition-payers.

A lot of 1Ls think about transferring, and a few do. Some transfer for geographical reasons, such as to be closer to family, but most think about transferring because they want to transfer up. Because their undergrad GPAs and LSATs count for little, if anything, in the transfer process, many students think they can now get into the schools that rejected them for regular admission. The Law School Admission Council compiles data on every law school in the online Official Guide to ABA-Approved Law Schools (*http://officialguide.lsac.org*), which includes the number of transfers in and out. Some schools send more out than they take in (the University of Akron, for example, had five transfers in and eight out according to the 2009 report), while more prestigious schools are likely to take more in (the University of Michigan took 32 and sent 10). Far more students, though, will think about transferring than will actually transfer. I will briefly write about the transfer process of those trying to move up, but these same concepts and procedures can apply to those who are transferring only for geographical or personal reasons.

How It Works

Generally, you apply to transfer at the end of your first year. You need the kind of stuff you needed for your original law school applications (LSAT score, undergrad grades, personal statement, and maybe a résumé) plus letters of recommendation from law school professors, your 1L grades, your class rank, and something to demonstrate that you are a student in good standing. This puts you in the tricky position of needing your current school administration and faculty to help you bail on them. If your transfer application is unsuccessful or you decide to stay anyway, you run the risk of alienating the home school. A lot of professors, though, are pretty nice and understanding about it, especially if you have an explanation for why you want to transfer. Only one of the professors I asked for a letter made an effort to stop me from transferring, but he abandoned it when I cut him off to explain that I had decided not to enroll for fall classes and had missed the deadline at that school, so I was definitely leaving—this radical strategy forced me to put a lot of effort into my transfer applications, but I would not recommend it to others. I was in a unique situation at a school with a low *U.S. News* ranking and approximately a quarter of my class transferred out, with many of us landing at top-tier law schools.

The interplay between the deadline to apply to law schools as a transfer student and the date you actually get your first-semester transcripts or class rank can make you pretty nervous. I wrote my personal statements, secured my letters, and had everything ready to go in anticipation of grades coming out. The day grades came out, I sent my applications with an unofficial transcript and requested an official transcript be sent as soon as possible. It is a lot easier to move quickly when everything is ready ahead of time. I applied to several schools, and they responded over the course of the summer. The most prestigious school I applied to (Michigan) accepted me within a day or two of receiving my official transcripts. Lesser-ranked schools rejected me, but I did not care because I had already heard from my first choice. I have heard of others, though, who did not get a response to transfer applications until the end of the summer and were essentially forced to make a last-minute decision on whether to move across the country. If accepted, you will have to go through some of the same processes you did as a 1L (putting down a deposit, applying for financial aid, and possibly attending some kind of orientation), but possibly on shorter notice and in a hurry.

Probably the biggest factors influencing your chance of acceptance are your class rank, where you go to law school, and your background (including your 1L summer job). Class rank in particular matters because schools use such different curves that GPAs are hard to read. At one school a student could have a 4.0 and be 10th in her class while a student at another school could be 1st with a 3.7. Generally, the higher the jump you are trying to make between law schools, the better your class rank must be. If you are trying to go from a low-ranked school to an elite school, you should be in at least the top 10 percent of your class. If the jump is not so dramatic, they might be content with a top-25-percent ranking. And transferring laterally to a school of equivalent prestige is possible when you're at or above the middle of the class. That you can transfer, though, does not mean you should.

Should You Transfer?

Before going through the transfer application process, you should think long and hard about why you want to transfer and whether it is worth it. If you are going to practice in the area of your current school, it is usually better to stay there—if you are going to law school in Nebraska, going to a more prestigious coastal school might not really help you get a job in Omaha. Every area has a regional school bias, and degrees from elite schools (especially with middle-of-the-road grades) might be insufficient to overcome that bias. But if you want to go to a top law firm in a big city that only hires students from top-twenty law schools or you aspire to become a law professor, transferring up might be worth it.

Think about the cost difference too. Do you have scholarships at your current law school? If not, do your 1L grades qualify you for a scholarship at your own school? (You can press your school to give you a scholarship to keep you from transferring.) Generally, transfer students are ineligible for scholarships at the transfer school, although a friend won a small scholarship from a West Coast school as an incentive to keep him from going to Michigan, and Michigan provided members of my transfer class with need-based aid.

If you are a top student looking to trade up, keep in mind that the competition at the new school will be tougher—you will be thrown into a pool of people just as bright as you, or brighter, and quite possibly more driven—and your grades do not transfer with you. Almost all students who transfer up experience a drop in their grades, although I actually did better at the "tougher" school, and I know others with similar experiences. You will also lose your 1L support group, and then there's the annoyance of moving to a new city. Losing your connections with your 1L professors also puts you at a disadvantage for developing the relationships you need to land jobs and clerkships. And while your new law school might increase your career opportunities, it is no guarantor of success—you will go into the fall interview process with only your prior school's transcripts.

When trying to pick which schools to apply to or which offer to accept, you should make sure that that the school accepts all of your credits. The law review competition process for transfers also varies among schools. When I was applying as a transfer, some schools were very welcoming (Michigan, Texas, Pepperdine) and held a special competition for transfer students to join because the normal deadline had passed. Notre Dame, on the other hand, essentially required transfers to go through all the work of applying to law review before being admitted to the school.

Law review can be very important, so pay special attention to this and investigate it before applying to schools or accepting an offer. You probably will not have enough information to assess the social situation at a school, but many transfers report feeling left out, and some schools have a reputation (at least on blogs) for looking down on transfers. I transferred to a school with a group of three dozen other transfers, and we had our own special orientation and sense of community.

Although transferring worked out very well for me, it is possible things would have worked out better for me had I stayed at my original school. Transferring is not a decision to be made lightly.

Key Points

- Think carefully about why you are attending law school, whether it is working out for you, and make a reasoned decision whether to continue.

- Transferring at the end of your first year can be a way to get into and graduate from a school that is ranked higher than where you currently attend, and that you might not have been able to gain admission to when you first applied to schools. Or it can simply put you in a geographical location that you are more comfortable with for whatever reason.

- Class rank matters because of the difference in GPA determinations between schools.

Chapter 9

STUDENT ORGANIZATIONS, MOOT COURT, AND CLINICS

THE LAW SCHOOL EXPERIENCE IS MORE THAN JUST CLASSES AND JOB SEEKING. Extracurricular activities are an important supplement to classes. These activities provide opportunities to have fun, develop relationships, network, build skills, and pad your résumé. As always, it is important to strike a balance with your time. You do not want to become so involved in activities that they take away from your studies, but you do not want to have a blank résumé, appear boring, or graduate from law school without friends.

Generally, most of the extracurricular activities are for 2Ls and 3Ls, with 1Ls only attending events and running for positions at the end of the first year. First-years usually have an intramural moot court competition in their legal writing class. Some clubs have a 1L representative position, and most student governments have representation for the 1L class, but this chapter will focus mostly on 2Ls and 3Ls.

Student Organizations

There are a lot of student organizations you can join. Your school will probably have some kind of recruiting fair for 1Ls in which the various groups put up booths. There are service groups, ethnic and minority groups, ideological or political groups, groups focused on a particular type of law, and groups that have nothing to do with law. Some schools have more active student bodies than others.

Joining student organizations can help your career. Membership in an organization focused on a particular kind of law (e.g., the Intellectual Property Society

107

or the Criminal Law Society) shows your interest in that area if you apply to a firm specializing in that kind of law. But be aware that if you are the head of the Criminal Law Society and you apply to a commercial litigation firm, you might give the impression that what you really want to do is try criminal cases. Membership in these topic-specific groups can also help you keep informed about the field and present opportunities to network with speakers working in that field.

Ideological organizations—like the conservative/libertarian Federalist Society or liberal American Constitution Society—host numerous speakers and run excellent national conferences. People that share your ideology may like seeing it on your résumé, but those who disagree with you might hold it against you. Sometimes being a member of an ideological organization can help you if you apply for judicial clerkships with judges who share that ideology. Join an ideological organization because you share its values, but put it on your résumé when you think it is appropriate.

If you have joined a group for fun, then leave it at that and do not waste your time being strategic about it. But if you are looking to boost your résumé—because leadership almost always looks good—you should put some mental effort into it. The best leadership positions, from a career perspective, are chair of the group and the position that handles speakers. Because hosting speakers is one of the primary activities for many law school groups, being in charge of speakers lets you have a role in setting the voice of the group. It also puts you in a position to network with speakers and with your professors or the national organization, from whom you can get advice on which speakers to host. The work level of each position varies. Some jobs are really only titles; the secretary or vice president of a club may have few responsibilities. Being the vice president in charge of coordinating speakers, though, might get you as much of a reward as chairing the organization, but with less overall work. Learn about the structure of the clubs you are involved in and go from there.

Many student organizations elect their leadership positions by default—only one person shows up to run. It is a lot easier to be the default choice than to face a real election. After joining the organization and getting involved, chat with the outgoing leadership before the election and find out if someone has the inside track. Ask them what is open and get their advice about positions. Figure out which 3L officers are graduating and which 2L officers are returning. If a 3L is chair and a 2L is vice-chair, that might tell you something.

But if the vote is contested, a little strategy goes a long way. If it is just an election, start by figuring out who can vote, when the vote takes place, and where it is held. The best way to get people to vote for you is to ask them to. Talk to group members individually and ask them specifically to vote for you. Then make sure you get your supporters to come to the meeting and remind them of the time. If this does not work, then make your other friends join the club to vote for you if needed.

Whatever position you end up in, do a good job as a matter of personal pride and as a way to make a name for yourself. If you are the treasurer, keep the books well. If you are the chair, lead the group well. Here are some suggestions:

- Recruit new members into the organization.
- Plan for a transition (i.e., start finding your replacement) from the start.
- Raise the profile of your group on campus through better advertising and more events.
- Promote the social aspect of the group and develop friendships within it, not just between yourself and the members but among others.
- Host interesting speakers.
- Host speakers well:
  - ◆ Provide lunch and, if possible, provide a good lunch.
  - ◆ Pick interesting or controversial talks.
  - ◆ Pick good speakers, and coordinate with other law schools nearby when you think arranging multiple stops will help get an out-of-state speaker more interested in your school.
  - ◆ Pick the right-size room. A room that cannot hold everyone is a disaster, but a giant 300-person lecture hall with 50 students spaced out throughout the room looks disappointing. Based on your estimated attendance, try to find a room that just barely holds everyone and will feel full.
  - ◆ Aggressively promote the speaker using any method possible (send e-mail, stuff student mailboxes, post flyers, ask professors to announce the lecture in his or her classes).
  - ◆ Use debates or panels to draw more attendance than lectures.
  - ◆ Invite a professor at your school who has a loyal student following to participate.
- Make your school look good to the national organizations and visiting speakers that you host.

Student Government

Law school student government is a kind of club. If you were a person who loved student government in high school or college, you might like this. If, on the other hand, you thought student government was a waste of time back then, you will probably find it an even bigger waste of time when you are sitting on committees with fellow law students. You can certainly tell which of those camps I fall into and where my bias lies. The time commitment varies by school and can be quite significant if your student government chooses to be particularly active.

One of my friends served during his 1L year and thinks it might have helped him land his 1L internship ("Who knows," he remarks), but he did not put much time into student government and does not even list it on his résumé. Many student government types claim that leadership positions in student government help students with average-to-decent grades compete for jobs, as it demonstrates that they can handle multiple responsibilities while still keeping their grades up. At a few schools the student government's top leadership receives a tuition subsidy, which is pretty cool, but that is uncommon. And even in those circumstances, student government is really only worth it when you value the service.

If you decide to run for student government, start by talking to people and simply being friendly. Those who talk to and relate with others on a friendly basis—those who do not seem overly competitive or arrogant but are just students—tend to win. Make good campaign flyers, preferably in two colors, with your last name in big, bold letters that people can read, but make sure that you do not violate any silly campaign rules and get yourself in trouble.

Clinics

Clinical programs are a popular and growing part of law schools. Some law schools have only one clinic to provide free or reduced-cost legal services to the less fortunate, while others have multiple, specialized clinics. Specialized clinics might do things like help low-income taxpayers, help small businesses fill out the necessary legal paperwork, handle criminal appeals, try to free allegedly innocent convicts, assist children in court, provide legal representation for immigrants, or litigate environmental issues. More general clinics serve the poor in a variety of ways.

Some clinics operate as classes that students can take for credit, while others are truly extracurricular. Some clinics take a tremendous amount of time and are very big deals in terms of prestige, workload, commitment, and relationship-building. Others are less intense and less fruitful in terms of experience and résumé-building. The real advantage in participating in a clinic is developing real legal experience and real skills while working for actual clients. Many students experience a degree of client contact in clinics that they might not achieve as a new attorney. Even if you do not plan to go into a clinic's particular field of law, the clinic can provide great general experience.

Actually going into court can build your confidence and set you up to go into court for different reasons. When I was at the University of Michigan, the school had a child advocacy clinic that billed itself as the clinic that went to court the most. Students were told that even if they did not want to do family law later in life, this was the clinic to be a part of if you wanted to be a litigator and be in court. I wish I had taken it.

Clinical faculty can also provide excellent references for future employers and, if your clinic requires you to write briefs or motions of some kind, the experience could produce a valuable writing sample. The final benefit of a clinic is that you might learn to love an area of law you are working in or realize that you hate a particular field, which can help you in selecting future classes and career paths.

I participated in Michigan's criminal appellate clinic, where I worked with the State Appellate Defender's Office on a collateral challenge to a prisoner's sentence. This clinic operated as a graded class and was not particularly time-intensive. I learned a lot, but it did not make a lasting impression on me or help me build friendships. Other friends participated in general clinics that required a lot more effort but carried a greater reward, and they are still in touch with other clinic alums. Like so many other things in law school, you get out of clinics what you put into them. I strongly recommend the clinic experience to almost any law student, especially those who might have less success in securing summer jobs and need to use clinics to put experience on their résumé, and those who plan on going solo after law school and crave practical experience.

The process of joining a clinic varies significantly by school. If it requires a personal statement or application, the advice provided in Chapter 10 on joining law reviews may be helpful. Attend any information sessions sponsored by the clinic and read its Web site and promotional material before crafting your personal statement so you will have an understanding of how it presents itself and what the clinic leaders are looking for in a member. Make sure you mind the deadlines. Some clinic deadlines are before the normal class selection process; you do not want to miss out. One last thing to watch for is prerequisites—for example, an environmental clinic may require you to take environmental law before applying.

Moot Court

Moot court and mock trial competitions simulate the courtroom experience in a competitive environment. Mock trial teams present a full case and often have the responsibility of bringing pretend witnesses as well. The American Bar Association also sponsors a client counseling competition in which law students simulate a meeting with a potential client to discuss legal problems. The most common type of simulation is moot court, which usually involves both an oral argument in front of an appellate tribunal and a brief. At top schools, the intramural competitions are often the most high-profile moot court. At many schools, teams may participate in an intramural competition to determine who will represent the school at state, regional, or national competitions. Some competitions vary topics every year, but others are topic-specific, focusing on intellectual property, environmental law, constitutional law, and so on.

Participating in moot court builds legal skills (although the skills are probably less practical than those picked up in clinics), self-confidence, and your résumé (much more so if you win). If you win at regional or national competitions, you also boost your school's pride. The public-speaking practice is almost certainly helpful, regardless of what area of law you are going into. You can also use moot court to show your interest in litigation or a particular subject matter—if you do the entertainment law moot court, that probably shows your interest in entertainment law to potential employers and to professors when you ask them to write letters of recommendations.

With moot court, I think it is helpful to look at the scoring sheets that are often provided along with the rules. Examine exactly how you are being judged and write your brief and structure your arguments accordingly. One of the keys to success is picking a good partner. Your partner can either bring you up or drag you down. It is important to find someone you can get along with, but the person needs to have the time to practice with you and get any written brief done far enough in advance of the deadline that you can integrate your respective portions into a workable single brief.

Many schools have an official moot court board. This group may organize intramural competitions or send teams off to represent the school in regional ones. The process for getting on the board varies and could involve a faculty nomination or an application. Being on the board is somewhat prestigious and looks good on a résumé, although it's perhaps not as good as actually winning a competition. If you want to be particularly strategic, you might consider picking a competition that you think you can win (something less popular, like the client counseling competition) as a résumé boost. All in all, moot court is a lot of work. I do not think it is worth doing just for the résumé; it is only worth it if you enjoy the competition and the arguments. I had a lot of fun participating in moot court, and if you think you will too, then give it a try.

Key Points

- If you are certain of a field of study you wish to practice in, joining a student organization focused on that particular kind of law can be helpful when applying to firms.
- Ideological organizations can be helpful if those seeing your résumé share your ideology, and hurt you if they do not. Join one that shares your values, but only put it on your résumé when you think it's appropriate.
- If you are looking for something to help your résumé, aim to become part of the leadership, such as a chair.
- Student government is an option, but gauge the time responsibilities against the career benefits.
- Clinics can be valuable tools to gain courtroom and legal experience (and help you decide a practice area you like), depending on the degree of intensity or exposure that the clinic provides, as well as garnish excellent references for future employers from the clinic faculty.
- Moot court and mock trial competitions build legal skills, self-confidence, and your résumé. But it is a significant amount of work, so you should also enjoy it, not just do it for the résumé boost.

Chapter 10

JOURNALS AND
LAW REVIEWS

LAW REVIEWS ARE ACADEMIC JOURNALS THAT PUBLISH SCHOLARLY PAPERS from professors, practitioners, and law students. With a few exceptions, legal journals are student-edited. Unlike most professions, where peer-review is the norm in scholarly journals, the legal field trusts students to select which articles to publish, edit those articles, and verify the research. While this practice has been criticized in some circles, it remains the norm. As a general rule, students are selected for the journal at the end of their first year and become associate editors their second year. Associate editors perform the grunt work of citation checking—ensuring that footnotes meet the requirements of the *Bluebook* and that the cited source supports the assertion. At the end of their 2L year, associate editors may run for editorial board positions and actually run the journal during their 3L year.

Joining a law journal has at least some potential to help you develop skills. It will expose you to scholarly writing, force you to learn most of the *Bluebook* rules for proper citation of authority, and could help you as a writer. While the requirements for scholarly writing are somewhat different from those for documents you file in court, developing good habits with your citations will make your future legal work easier and better. The primary advantage to working on a journal, though, is prestige. Attorneys often include their past journal memberships in their law-firm bios for the rest of their lives. Journal membership is very important if you are thinking of applying for judicial clerkships. Many schools have secondary journals in addition to their flagship law review. My law school had a particularly large number, including specialty journals focused on race, gender, technology, law reform, and international law.

Membership in a school's main law review is much more prestigious, and you should aim for that if possible. Some secondary journals are more prestigious than others, but outside of your classmates and legal academics, most people probably will not know which specialty journals are higher-ranked. It is best to apply to any journal you would be willing to join. If you are invited to join more than one, you should take the main law review over a secondary journal almost every time—only pick a secondary journal if you are certain what kind of law you want to go into, the journal fits that field exactly, and you are not concerned about prestige. And if you have to choose among secondary journals, pick the one whose topic area and people interest you the most, unless prestige is of particular importance in the career track you selected.

The application process varies. At some schools, grades alone are enough to get on the journal, with those crossing a certain threshold (say, the top 10 percent of the class) automatically making law review, although the trend might be away from this. At a few schools, secondary journals also have automatic admission based on grades (e.g., the top 33 percent get an offer to join the secondary journal, or students with an A in Intellectual Property are offered the chance to join the IP journal). Still others consider grades but also place a heavy emphasis on a writing competition. Others consider only an applicant's writing and require a writing sample, personal statement (more common for special secondary journals), and note proposal. The process should be made clear to you toward the end of your 1L year. By the time you work on law-review applications after your 1L exams, it is too late to boost your grades (if those are a part of the process), so I will focus on how to build a better application and writing sample.

Getting on Law Review

Law-journal writing competitions are usually held in the weeks after the end of 1L exams. This means that you have to find time to take on a significant additional project immediately after completing your 1L year. It is a daunting task, but be aware of the deadlines and find the time to do it. Make sure you do not schedule a trip or a move in such a way that it keeps you from building an application, and keep this in mind when setting the start date for your 1L summer job. Like so many things in law school, you are effectively graded against your peers. Law journals generally have a set number of members they are looking for, and you need to rank high enough in their preferences to land an offer to join.

Your writing competition packet will usually be graded by the rising 3Ls who have recently been elected to the journal's editorial board. They might manage it so that a few members of the editorial board grade all of the applications, or they might have each member grade a handful. When preparing your application materials, keep your audience in mind. These are busy students who have already completed a year on a journal. Make sure you get the easy points and do not lose ground for stupid mistakes. Your graders are used to spotting and fixing errors. Proofread your entry again and again. Their journal experience has given them a working knowledge of the *Bluebook*. Make sure you know whether to underline or italicize the period after "*Id.*", as you can bet your graders do. One important thing to remember is that those who will be making the decisions on membership are not that much smarter or more educated than those applying. In general, they know the *Bluebook* extremely well, so that is where most of your focus should be. You have to include some sort of analysis, but the cleverest analysis may not be recognized by those with the power to grant you membership.

If your application packet calls for a personal statement, you should take this seriously. Unless you know from some public grading guidelines that the personal statement is worth little, put a lot of work into it. Be convincing, and make sure you write well. Personal statements can really distinguish candidates. They are always hard, and the best way to prepare yourself is to research the journal. If the journal has an information session, attend it, take notes on what they are saying, and then write out in your own words exactly what they said they are looking for in applicants. If they do not have a session like that, at least visit the journal's Web site to see what it does and read its mission statement. In other words, find out what the board wants to hear from applicants, and then say that with as much honest detail as you can. You need to say something more than that you heard law review will look good on your résumé. Saying that you are interested in writing a note (a student paper published in the law review) shows that you want to work hard and have a grasp of what academic journals do (they publish scholarly papers).

The standard law review write-on contest involves a closed-universe problem. This means that the editorial board gives you a set number of sources (cases, law-review articles, newspapers, and so on) from which to construct a serious academic paper. Do a great job on this writing task. Make sure your structure, style, and substance are top-notch. Broader advice on legal writing is beyond the scope of this book, but if you are serious, I highly recommend that you read Eugene Volokh's *Academic Legal Writing*. I will offer one serious tip: When planning your time, make sure you leave time to put as much work into revising the entry as into writing it.

For guidance on note proposals, first read Chapter 12 about choosing paper topics and writing good papers. Selecting a good topic is the key to demonstrating you understand what is involved with publishing a scholarly journal. Make sure your proposal establishes why your topic matters. If there is a circuit split and nobody else has written on the topic, say so. If it is becoming increasingly important, explain why. And try to be original—when I was grading applications for a technology secondary journal, a surprisingly large number of proposals all concerned a law Congress had just passed limiting online poker.

Some competitions, more commonly among secondary journals, permit you to submit a writing sample that was developed for something else. Generally, students use their entries in the primary law-review competition or a brief of memo from their legal writing class. Use your very best work. If you use something from a legal writing class, revise it further. Take advantage of the professor's notes and comments to improve it. Put some extra effort into revising and editing it. If you are extremely confident in your primary law-review entry, you can use that instead, although you run the risk of being overconfident with a bad entry and striking out with all the journals.

Making the Editorial Board

The outgoing editorial board elects its replacements from among the journal's 2L associate editors. The election process and degree of formality vary significantly among journals. But in all such situations, the senior editors on your journal have to like you and respect you. The first step to achieving this is doing good work. For 2Ls, this usually means doing your cite-checking correctly. Invest the time to learn the *Bluebook* rules and how to apply them. Once you know how to do it, the work will go more quickly. Always be on time in your cite-checking and any other project they give you—on time doesn't mean five minutes late. If you are consistently late, even just by a couple of minutes, it will work against you. You should cultivate a reputation for getting everything in early and, if you can handle the work, asking if there is anything else you can do. Learn from the process: Follow up to find out what mistakes you made and avoid those mistakes in the future. If you find a problem in an article, do not simply flag it for the senior editor; flag it and offer a helpful solution. Take that same attitude into other things the journal does. If they need volunteers to staff a booth at an alumni event, volunteer a little bit of your time. If your journal hosts a symposium, attend at least some of it.

Work the personal angles as well. Attend social events and talk to the upper-classmen. If you have nothing worthwhile to talk about, then ask them for advice. Ask your editor-in-chief about his or her job prospects or why he or she is taking a clerkship, and then ask for advice on the clerkship application process. When the application process is approaching, ask the person who has the job you most want to meet with you so you can solicit his or her advice. Valuing somebody's advice can be a very effective form of flattery, but it should also be sincere, as it will help you do the job better if you get it. If your journal requires you to write out some kind of statement or fill out an application form, keep the audience in mind as you write it. Write what you think will sway these people, and get input and editorial help from your friends (unless that is prohibited).

Finally, do not give up. I did a terrible job with cite-checking. One of my projects in the fall was a few hours late. But I was able to turn around my reputation sufficiently by the time editorial board elections were held in the spring to earn the number-two spot on the journal for my 3L year.

The structure and titles of editorial boards varies by journal and by school. Different schools call the same job different things or divide responsibilities differently. The names may change, but the duties are typically the same. Generally, journals that publish more issues will have larger editorial boards. At the risk of oversimplification, here is a sketch of the kind of editorial board positions that might be available:

- Editor-in-chief. This is the number-one person on the journal, responsible for managing it and making final decisions, and who may have a significant role in article selection and editing. This is a very time-consuming position.
- Managing editor. This is the number-two person on the journal. The managing editor usually handles the business, organizational, and membership responsibilities of the journal, with varying degrees of editorial involvement.
- Executive editor. Most journals have some senior position that supervises note and article editors and handles a second level of editing.

- Article or note editor. This person handles the first round of editing law-review articles and is usually responsible for inputting changes produced by the associate editors who review the footnotes. Typically, this person works with authors directly, and authors will develop an impression about the journal based on their interaction with the article editor.
- Submissions editor. While the title may vary, almost every journal has some person with the job of sifting through the hundreds or thousands of submissions that law journals get each year.
- Symposium editor, blog editor, etc. Depending on what kind of other activities a journal has, somebody will be responsible for them and probably be called an editor, even if he or she does very little editing.

Publishing and Making the Most of Your Journal Experience

Law reviews are in the business of publishing, but most law students never publish a student law-review note. Some journals require every member to write a note and publish a few of them. Other journals have no note requirement and thus receive fewer submissions, and they publish just about everything they receive. If you are going to do the work of writing a long academic paper, you might as well get the recognition of publishing it.

If you are going to publish a paper, you have to write publishable-quality work on a publishable topic. This means writing about something that is relevant and taking a position that nobody else has (so that your paper is not preempted) while writing a well-researched scholarly paper. For a discussion of note topics, see Chapter 12. The hardest part is motivation. If your journal does not have a note requirement, it is hard to motivate yourself to put in the work, but it might be easier to get your note published if there are fewer submissions. If your journal has a nominal requirement or clearly does not intend to publish all of the submissions, it might be hard to motivate yourself to take your 10-page paper that meets the minimum requirements and turn it into 25 pages of graduate-level scholarship worthy of publication in an academic journal. My suggested approach is to double up on motivation. Take a seminar class with a paper-writing requirement and plan from the beginning to use that seminar paper as your note. The motivation to publish the paper will help you put that tiny bit of extra work into the class, resulting in a higher grade, and will leave you with a great note to submit to your journal.

Outside of publishing, there are a few other things you can do to make the most of your law review experience. You can make the most of the human contacts by meeting professors and practitioners at symposiums, events, or meals your journal puts together and by getting to know your fellow editors more deeply to create a lifelong network. You can actually take in the scholarship by reading the material your journal puts out. You can contribute to that scholarship not only by publishing your own but also by blogging about it and participating in your journal's own blog, if it has one. And finally, you can make an effort to promote and publicize your journal. The better and more prestigious it becomes, the better it looks on your résumé.

Key Points

- Legal journals are generally student-edited, with few exceptions.
- Apply to any journal you have an interest in joining.
- The school's main law review is the most prestigious of their journals.
- Edit and proofread your application and submissions many times.
- Take any requirement for a personal statement seriously. Do not brush it off.
- Read Eugene Volokh's *Academic Legal Writing*.
- Put as much work into revising an entry as it took to write it.
- Always be on time and show up at social events if you are interested in making it onto the editorial board.

Chapter 11

Writing Seminar Papers and Notes

Picking a Topic

Your goal is to pick a topic that lends itself to real, thoughtful, original, graduate-level thinking about a subject you have an interest in. Picking a good topic makes writing a paper easier, and a paper with a truly great topic sometimes seems to write itself. You should find a legal problem and try to solve it. Preferably, you should find a topic that no one else has written about or offer a new solution to a problem others have identified, although some professors might not emphasize novelty in seminar papers. The best way to start this process is by being open-minded to the potential paper topics all around. When you pay attention to the news and see that the president pardoned someone only to revoke the pardon a few days later, this might jump out to you as a potential paper topic on presidential power. Think about the legal implications of everyday situations, such as adult children moving back in with their parents and whether parents would have legal authority to consent to a police search of their children's stuff. You can see paper topics in the reading you do for class, whether in the footnotes in the cases or the editorial notes that follow the cases.

Watch for paper topics in the issues you confront in summer jobs, externships, and clinics. Look for rules that are unclear with no cases to explain them or new statutes whose impact is unclear. The things that confused you—places where there is a hole in the law—probably confuse others too and probably could use some thoughtful analysis. National issues, though, often make better topics than local ones.

The classic idea for a paper topic is a circuit split—the situation in which one of the federal circuit courts interprets something one way and at least one other circuit comes out with the opposite interpretation of the same statute, case, rule, or constitutional provision. By their very nature, circuit splits have a body of writing and thinking on them already developed, if only in the appellate court's opinions. They are inherently relevant because under a circuit split, the outcome of a lawsuit depends on the court a person files suit in. These kinds of situations are often resolved by the U.S. Supreme Court. Writing about a circuit split is the classic kind of student paper; it works well, but it is somewhat clichéd. If you are hoping the paper will be published and maintain relevancy in the long run, writing about a circuit split runs the risk that the Supreme Court will resolve the issue and make your paper seem outdated.

Writing about Supreme Court cases has its own kind of peril. If you write about a pending Supreme Court case, your writing could be shallow and might look foolish if the case is resolved in a way contrary to your analysis. If you want to write about a Supreme Court case, it might be better to cover the application of principles from a very recent case to a new set of facts or pending cases. For instance, the Supreme Court held in *Wyeth v. Levine* that FDA regulations on what drug-makers could put on warning labels did not preempt tort suits based on injuries caused by a drugmaker's failure to include information on warning labels. One student wrote a paper immediately after *Wyeth* about the implication of that case on litigation involving makers of generic drugs, who are required by the FDA to run the exact same warning labels as the pioneer drugmaker, with a reference to how this should impact pending litigation in lower courts. This idea made for an excellent, relevant, and timely paper.

She got the idea by talking to her professor. Law professors are scholars—they write academic papers and come up with ideas for a living. They can be great sources of ideas, but there are also risks in asking a professor for an idea. Depending on their maturity level, they might be unhappy if you reject their idea. You also run the risk of taking the professor's idea and writing about it in a different way or with a different outcome from what the professor expects. You might get great points for challenging the professor's thinking, or he or she might think you are simply wrong. Nevertheless, you should always try to get your professor's feedback on a topic. He or she might know why it is a bad idea, how to structure the paper, or where to go for more information. When I told one professor I wanted to write about online defamation, he told me it was an interesting, timely topic, but he also warned me that there was a tremendous body of literature on the topic. If you choose to write about something others have written about, he warned, you have to come up with an original idea or a novel approach, which can be hard when so much has already been written. I was able to do so, and he commended me on the approach I developed.

If you have not stumbled upon an idea, there are many ways to look for one. You can start by asking smart and creative friends, bosses, or coworkers. If they have been paying attention to case developments or the news, they might have their own suggestions. A potentially great way to find topics is by reading idea-focused law blogs, such as the Volokh Conspiracy (*http://www.volokh.com*), Concurring Opinions (*http://www.concurringopinions.com/*), PrawfsBlawg (*http://prawfsblawg.blogs.com/*), or Mirror of Justice (*http://www.mirrorofjustice.blogs.com/*). There are also a variety of topic-specific blogs, such as Sentencing Law and Policy (*http://sentencing.typepad.com/*) and Religion Clause (*http://religionclause.blogspot.com/*). You can look for a law blog on the topic your class is covering and see the recent developments and issues in that field. When reading posts on these ideas-focused blogs, it might also be worth it to look at the comments on those posts. The comments often come from other professors with interesting thoughts. If you are a liberal or progressive student, the American Constitution Society provides a whole Web site of interesting topics for liberal law students to write papers about (*http://researchlink.acslaw.org/*). You might also find ideas for unresolved topics from treatises, practice aids, and legal newspapers.

To find your own circuit splits, run a search in LexisNexis or Westlaw's federal case database with something like "circuit w/2 split!" and a recent date range (such as the last two years). Add a search phrase relevant to your class—e.g., "and 'religious accommodation'" or "w/50 'religious accommodation'"—to try to make the results more relevant to your class.

I cannot stress how important it is to pick a good topic. Even with great writing, a weak topic can only carry a paper so far, and you might find yourself 15 pages into a 25-page paper with nothing left to discuss and not enough time to start from scratch. I took several "paper classes" in law school—classes where I had to write a final paper instead of an exam—and the struggles I had with my worst paper primarily came from picking a poor topic. I picked one that was not relevant enough and had very few outside sources to draw on. After I proved my point, I had nobody else's arguments to counter. It was not a disaster, but it was way harder than it needed to be and the grade was not exactly what I wanted. Unless your professor tells you otherwise, writing a paper that is simply a response to someone else, identifying a problem but failing to offer a solution, or merely explaining the law without solving a problem, usually makes for a poor seminar paper. And a poor paper can often be surprisingly difficult to write.

Legal Research for Academic Papers

While an important topic and snazzy writing are important, research forms the backbone of your analysis and is one of your key contributions to legal scholarship. Student papers are rarely cited for their analytical contributions, but they are regularly cited for their research. In this section I focus only on legal research, and even then only with the big legal databases, and I offer relatively simple advice. Legal scholars are increasingly turning to multidisciplinary research, but most student scholarship continues to rely on basic legal research. Because the technology and interface of the legal research Web sites are continually evolving, I will cover the principles to apply in legal research rather than the nuts and bolts of how to search.

Learning the Nuts and Bolts

First, you need to learn the nuts and bolts of how to search. Attend all of the seminars that Westlaw and LexisNexis put on at your school. Many of them will offer a free lunch and promotional points you can redeem for goods or gift cards. When you are at this training, take and keep all of the handouts. You might not use the particular skill—legislative history research, for example—right away and might forget what you learned. But the handout can refresh your memory, or simply walk you through the research process, if you need to use the skills later.

You should also take advantage of the people at your school who are paid to help you research. Westlaw and LexisNexis both pay student representatives to keep hours in your library. Find out who those people are and come to them with research problems and questions. Do not try to get them to do the work for you, but ask them to show you the right way to do things. Your law librarians are also there to help you research, and they will have familiarity with the more obscure databases, such as those housing historical documents. But many people find the Westlaw and LexisNexis reps more approachable, and if your searches are confined to purely legal topics, fellow students might suffice.

As you learn to use the database systems, you will have to learn to make your searches more efficient. Often this involves finding the right words. I wrote a paper about state and federal regulation of robocalls, which are automated political phone calls. Most states have some kind of regulation that affects automated calls, but they often use different words to describe the same thing. I had to continually update my search string by looking through the statutes I did find and the neighboring statutes within the same part of that code. Other times I updated the wording of my search after reading cases or other law review articles. It is somewhat obvious if your search is too broad—it will have too many results—but if your search is too narrow and has too few results, you might not know that's the problem. A little common sense is important in choosing your wording—something like "the right to be a candidate" might be described someplace else as "the right to run for public office"—and it sometimes helps to search broadly at first and then narrow the results. It can also be helpful to do a quick Google or Wikipedia search, in order to get a better idea of the different terms used to express a particular idea. That can then inform your choice of search terms.

Researching

One way to start your research is by finding everything written about your topic and at least skimming through or reading the section that covers your topic to decide if it is relevant. Keep all of the relevant material and find a way to organize it. I tend to keep one or more computer files with my raw research, which I later copy and paste from into my writing. Others print, highlight, and sort the physical piles of paper. There are some constraints on how many articles you can keep in physical form. However, if the stack starts getting too tall, it might be a signal that your research topic is too broad. When you go through law review articles and secondary sources, check the footnotes of those articles to find more articles and cases to read. A tip for reading law review articles: After you have used a research tool to find them, you might want to actually view or print the PDFs from HeinOnline (a service your law school undoubtedly subscribes to), which gives you a much more readable format with the footnotes at the bottom of each page.

You also want to find all of the cases that matter to your topic. Once you find the right case, regulation, or statute, run a KeyCite in Westlaw or Shepardize it. Be sure to note any negative treatment as well as the precise reason for the negative treatment, as a case can be overruled on one point while remaining good law for other principles. It is always important to try to read all of the cases, but it is particularly important in scholarly writing because one case can lead you to other cases and jurisdictions, introduce you to new doctrines, and help you develop better search terms. Read all of the cases, within reason. If you are writing about federal sentencing under Section 3553(a), too many cases will come up and you will have to limit yourself to Supreme Court cases or add a specific search term to focus the results.

Finally, do not let Westlaw or LexisNexis blind you—not everything is in a legal research database. You should also try Googling some of the things you are writing about to make sure you do not miss a major development or news item, and you can also use Google to search legal blogs (particularly those written by professors), which are becoming increasingly important. They are cited in court opinions and law review articles, are often very timely, and sometimes provide excellent analysis of the topic. You can also find law review articles via Google before they are actually published and available in the legal databases. Professors often post working drafts of their papers on the Social Science Research Network (SSRN). These papers may be helpful and worth citing, but they might also convince you to back away from your topic if someone else is already saying the exact same thing.

Writing the Paper

Seminar papers are usually expected to be graduate-level scholarship. This requires a good deal of effort and some actual planning. For many students, this might be the longest and most difficult paper they will ever write. Others may not find it challenging at all. The paper is likely to be longer than the brief you wrote for your legal writing class, but it is different in other ways too.

Seminar papers delve much deeper into policy arguments and address broader issues—you do not have to try for the minimalist approach that is necessary for good briefs. You get to challenge existing law, and not just a single statute—you can attack big doctrines if you have reason and the courage to. I would not suggest attacking the doctrine of judicial review espoused in *Marbury v. Madison*, but if you think affirmative action is always unconstitutional or that bans on affirmative action are unconstitutional, these are arguments you can successfully make in a scholarly paper, despite the Supreme Court's nuanced and contrary rulings. If your paper is too controversial, though, you could anger your professor and eliminate its value as a writing sample.

Scholarly writing also treats counterarguments seriously and with respect, rather than seeking to marginalize or defeat those arguments. Unless otherwise instructed, your citations should be in footnotes rather than in the text (as they usually are in briefs). And not only will they include footnotes, they will include a lot of them—but do not take the footnote thing too far. One of my friends dropped a footnote in a published paper to cite the Constitution for the proposition that Congress makes federal laws. If the reader will already know that the claim within the sentence is correct, the source is obvious, and specificity is unnecessary, leave the footnote out. Scholarly writers often use footnotes as places to stash additional ideas, such as comments on a case or limits on certain arguments or proposals. Using footnotes for this purpose can be fun, but do not use it excessively—some of the law review articles you read during research might do this and should not be imitated. Generally a footnote should be used in this manner only if putting it in the text would completely disrupt the flow of the current topic. Of course, if it can be expanded into a separate topic within the same paper, it should go there, rather than in a footnote.

In many legal writing classes, the rules strictly forbid you to consult with outsiders or have others look over your work. With seminar papers, you might be allowed to receive feedback from others, giving credit for their help where appropriate, which can greatly improve your writing.

As with other types of writing, the best way to start down the path to proficiency is to read good writing. If you have time, try to read a paper authored by your professor. Pay attention to your professor's style, including his or her footnoting style. At the very least, read one or two of the articles you turn up in your research. And I mean actually read them start to finish, paying attention to the structure and the style, rather than just grabbing the quotes and information you need. But keep in mind that there are a lot of poorly written law review articles out there.

Do not let the highbrow arguments or complex nature of a topic tempt you into writing overly wordy junk. As with your other writing assignments, it is important to write well, with crisp, clean sentences. Do not use big words, technical jargon, or passive voice just because you think it makes you sound smart. Instead, actually be smart by picking your words well. Rather than trying to replicate the many fine books that instruct you in solid writing (such as Eugene Volokh's *Academic Legal Writing*), this section will give you a heads-up on the basic structure of seminar papers, offer advice on how to approach the writing, and help you avoid some common pitfalls. If you have already picked a decent topic and performed solid research, you are in a good position to start writing the paper.

The basic format of a seminar paper is to take a position and then support it. You might argue that a statute is unconstitutional and should be replaced with another, show examples of why it is unconstitutional when applied, respond to the arguments of those who say it is constitutional, and then show why your proposal is both constitutional and works well within the examples you used earlier. Keep this general format in mind as you go about the process of organizing your paper.

For your first seminar paper, the best way to start the process is to start with the research. Pull all the quotes, statutory sections, arguments, counterarguments, and ideas you come across into one computer document of notes—this will end up being a very big file. Then as you go about writing the paper, cut and paste the tidbits of research into another document where you can do the actual writing. This means that when you finish your first draft, it will be a relatively complete paper, mostly in need of language tweaks rather than additional research. You can also use your notes or research file as a place to dump spontaneous ideas as they come to you over the course of the semester, plugging them into your paper as you edit it.

Some legal writers do the exact opposite—they write the paper first and then fill in the sources. They just drop blank footnotes and fill them in later (or, because these are usually professors, they have research assistants fill them in). Writing this way works when you really understand the law well—when your expert knowledge allows you to write something knowing that sources out there will back it up. For your first paper, I suggest doing the research first and plugging it in as you write. As you do so, you must be meticulous about giving proper attribution to your sources. There is very little that will get you in as much trouble as plagiarism, even if it is unintentional.

Once your research is put together, it helps to develop an outline so that your paper has a logical structure to it and you have a starting place to begin your com-position. As in a brief, section headings help you to organize your paper and your thinking. You can put them in place and start to write around them. I often wrote the section headings (or at least a rough draft of them), copied the raw information from my research file below the headings, and then converted the material into readable prose one subsection after another. Your actual headings should not be as argumentative as those in a brief, but they should be more descriptive than merely "Precedent."

Content

The analysis section is the meat of your paper, and you should probably write it first, then your introduction, and then your conclusion. Some write the introduction first, but you will have to plan on rewriting it after the analysis is in place. Otherwise you will impose unfair constraints on your own imagination and creativity if you demand that your paper follow what your original introduction said. Once you start writing the analysis section, you need to clearly and strongly take a position. Your paper should solve a problem, which requires either creating the problem yourself and convincing the reader along the way, or showing that others find it a problem in a way that convinces the reader to share their concern. The position you take should be as good as your topic in terms of novelty and value to the legal profession—which is to say, do not come up with a ridiculous solution to a good problem. Unless your professor tells you otherwise, make sure you solve a problem:

- Do not just identify problems without giving an answer.
- Do not just explain the law.
- Do not just respond to someone else's article.

Newspapers can provide you with fresh examples to show why this is such a problem. You might consider creating a Google News Alert to give you a heads-up on new examples in case they come up over the course of the semester after you stop researching. This way you will get an e-mail (you can choose whether you receive it weekly or daily) anytime a story appears about your topic (e.g., an alert for "Hatch Act violation" or "Texas polygamy"). Real examples help to drive home the significance of your paper and prove the value of your solution. If you cannot find real examples, you can make up hypothetical situations that show the absurdity of existing law, another commentator's proposal, or counterarguments to your ideas, and that demonstrate the rationality of your resolution of the problem. A good set of hypotheticals, if they are comprehensive, can make for a very good paper. It takes a lot of time to come up with a comprehensive list, and you will want to have a bunch of people look over your list to make sure you have not duplicated or missed anything. Make sure your hypotheticals are realistic, though. If they seem too far-fetched or too perfect, their persuasive effect will be limited.

Not every situation, real or hypothetical, that you test your proposal on needs to reach a perfect result. But if the result seems odd, you should explain why. The uncertainties can be very helpful in describing where more research needs to be done or where the law is lacking. Either way, these explanations can be just as important as your actual conclusions. The impact of practical considerations or other laws might place limits on your proposal, so you should clearly state and explain these. For example, a young scholar I know recently wrote a paper arguing that the Constitution's Free Exercise Clause requires an exemption from polygamy laws for people whose religion requires that they practice polygamy. He provided an example of nonreligious polygamists (he worked hard to make that feel realistic), recognized that his proposal would help the religious but not the secular, and concluded that the Constitution created that distinction and, basically, tough luck for the secular polygamist. In scholarly legal writing, your ideas do not have to be perfect, but your paper needs to recognize and discuss its own imperfections.

Your analysis section will typically start with the background of facts or law of your issue. Do not get bogged down too much in its history, unless the history is actually relevant (if your proposed resolution turns on the legislative history, for example) or very interesting. It is very tempting to spend too much time on history because you can fill pages with it. However, it is only rarely useful for understanding the current problem and, unless you have a history background, you may make simple mistakes that will look bad.

Let the problem you propose to solve show through in the background section, if applicable. Now prove the proposition that forms the basis of your paper. The real-world problems, cases, and hypotheticals you identified earlier should drive your writing and help to redefine your proposal as you write. You should recognize counterarguments to the points you make and take them on head-on. Showing how your ideas and analysis hold up against counterarguments strengthens your proposal and shows that it is well thought-out.

Identify counterproposals (which might be the existing law, different ways courts resolved an issue on which there is a circuit split, or arguments raised by professors in law review articles) and show how they fail. Test your proposal on the real-world examples that you came up with, test counterproposals on them, and show how your resolution is more reasonable. If there is some underlying theory behind your proposal, explain it, and if you can connect your idea to bigger issues, do so. In two papers I wrote in law school about election-related topics, I showed that regulations I did not like tended to protect incumbents and connected my proposals to the broader issue of competitive elections. It is important, also, to acknowledge the limits of your proposal if it is inapplicable in some situations.

After you have put together your analysis section, either rewrite your introduction or create it for the first time. Your intro should show readers there is a problem before briefly mentioning your solution and offering a road map for the rest of your paper. It is particularly important to show readers the problem right upfront in a way that catches their attention. Start with a scary statistic, a dangerous-sounding example, or a laundry list of problems. Here is the first paragraph of a paper that I wrote for a class and later published (see the section on publishing later in this chapter):

> It happens prior to every election. An employee of a local or state government agency decides to run for political office on the employee's own time only to find out that he will lose his job if he actually files to run for office. What would have been an election fight turns into an employment dispute. Some choose to withdraw their candidacy, some choose to continue their races at the expense of their day job, while some are given no choice at all. The covered employees are put in this position because of a federal law called the Hatch Act. The Hatch Act's coverage of state and local government employees often comes as a surprise to those involved because the statute does not provide clear notice regarding who and what is actually covered. Even if the potential candidates are aware of federal grants coming into an agency, they think of themselves as state, not federal, employees and do not necessarily realize that federal grants make state employees answerable to the Hatch Act. If they are aware of the Hatch Act at all, they likely think of its coverage of federal—not state—employees, because the federal provisions are the ones that most often make news. All fifty states impose some restrictions on the political activities of government employees, and state workers may be more familiar with those provisions than the federal Hatch Act. When a covered employee files to run for office, he or she is usually given a choice—give up your campaign or give up your job—but the stigma of being "an illegal candidate" has nonetheless already attached.

The Unwise and Unconstitutional Hatch Act: Why State and Local Government Employees Should be Free to Run for Public Office, 34 S. Ill. U. L. J. 313-14 (2010).

You can see how I tried to make a law you probably never heard of before sound important and generate sympathy for my anti–Hatch Act point of view before actually stating my proposal. But leading with concrete examples can show the reader the problem, rather than just telling them. I started another paper like this:

> African-American voters receive a phone message implying that they are not registered to vote. Others hear "an almost threatening male voice," a "fake New York accent," factual distortions about legislation, false endorsements from controversial groups, calls promoting one candidate claiming to be from his opponent, and a constant barrage of annoying phone calls designed to make voters think a different candidate was sponsoring them. These messages were delivered through automated political telephone calls, also known as robocalls. Robocalls are cheap and efficient—one can deliver a prerecorded message through 100,000 automated phone calls in one hour for only $2000. Consequently, robocalls have become one of the most-used political campaign tools.

Note, *Regulating Robocalls: Are Automated Calls the Sound of, or a Threat to, Democracy?*, 16 Mich. Telecomm. Tech. L. Rev. 214-15 (2009).

Unlike my Hatch Act paper, this one opens with a string of real examples. Each of the examples I cite has a footnote giving the news story that is its source. Even if you have never heard a robocall, or heard of one, you see from real examples and news stories that others care about this problem. The string of examples plus footnotes helps to build credibility. You can accomplish the same thing, though, with a single compelling anecdote or statistic, or in any number of other ways. In another paper, I started by citing a newspaper story on multigenerational households and used the name of an individual the story focused on:

> Ann Brown lives with her 30-something daughter and granddaughter in a condo she owns. What would happen if the police suspected her daughter of some crime and asked Ann to consent to a search of her daughter's private bedroom? Would she have authority to consent to a search of her daughter's personal property within that bedroom? Police will face these questions with increasing frequency. An AARP survey earlier this year reported that 33 percent of respondents aged 18 to 49 lived with their parents or their spouse's parents. Experts predict that the

recent economic downturn will increase that number as adult children move in with their parents. Furthermore, the retirement of the baby boom generation may lead more parents to move in with their adult children. Courts will increasingly face the difficult question of whether a parent has authority to consent to the search of the adult child's private bedroom and property.

When Is a Parent's Authority Apparent? Reconsidering Third Party Consent Searches of an Adult Child's Private Bedroom and Property, 24 Crim. Just. 34-37 (Winter 2010) (citation omitted).

Having convinced you that the raw numbers of multigeneration households would make the legal questions more numerous and more important, I then went on to describe, in the next paragraph, the circuit split on this question and thus fully convince the reader that my topic mattered. My introductions are not exceptional, but they are passable, and I hope you can draw enough from them to write an even better start to your papers. Now that you have your analysis and introductory sections completed, turn to your conclusion.

The conclusion should briefly summarize your holding. It is a place the reader can look to when trying to figure out your ultimate holding and, simply put, just a way to end your paper. You do not need to be particularly beautiful or powerful here—it is not a custom of academic legal writing to end powerfully. But if you do have something really strong to say at the end of your conclusion, do so. Writing the conclusion and having someone else comment on it can be extremely helpful. Sometimes you will write your conclusion, summarizing what you think you have argued, only to find out that what a reader gets from your paper is something entirely different. Because you wrote the paper, your brain will often fill in gaps, so that the paper means one thing to you and another to the reader. The two should be as close as possible, so have someone read your paper and tell you whether the conclusion matches their impressions of the paper. If they do not match, you need to rewrite either the paper or the conclusion.

With any kind of legal writing, longer is not always better. That you can write up to thirty pages is not a reason to use thirty pages. Law school seminar papers are not like undergrad papers—do not add fluff to your paper just to make it longer. Exactly how long your paper should be is a hard line to draw. Fit in everything you need to, and plan on vigorously cutting out unnecessary thoughts and words during the editing process.

Editing and Titles

Plan on doing a lot of editing after your rough draft is done, which means you shouldn't put off completing the paper until the end of the semester (as many undergrads do). Start editing your paper right away, but budget time to come back to it later with a fresh set of eyes. Early in the semester, ask your professor if he or she will look over a draft if it is turned in early. And find out exactly when early is for your professor, as he or she may have other obligations, such as writing the final exam for another class. If your professor will look over your paper, take him or her up on this. If you are too swamped, try to at least discuss an outline with the professor. After you get your professor's feedback on the rough draft, fixing it up according to his or her suggestions is a pretty good way to get a good grade. You are usually allowed to have others look over your seminar paper (the custom is to thank or recognize others for their input in the opening footnote), and if your school allows it, you should always take advantage of this. Your friends might see counterarguments or problems that you do not. They might have great ideas or simply tell you a section is unpersuasive. Similarly, if your school has a writing center where you can take a paper to get help, this too might be worthwhile to improve your language and erase some of the legalese. You should try to get your paper into as good a condition as possible before asking others to look at it, because the better the condition of your paper, the better the feedback you will get. For example, if you turn in a paper full of grammatical errors to your friends, they will likely point out the obvious grammatical errors rather than think deeply about your legal claim.

Your friends can also serve as a helpful sounding board for paper titles. I usually pick a tentative title when I start the paper—mostly because I want to have something in bold at the very top of my Microsoft Word document—and think seriously about the title at the end. Professors can be a great resource on this, too. I originally titled my robocalls paper *Robocalls and the First Amendment*, but my professor pointed out that I really was not focusing on the First Amendment very much but instead mostly on the regulatory structure, so the title shifted to *Regulating Robocalls*. I tend to make my titles too long, as you can see from the citations following those excerpts above, and I could have probably told the reader what the paper was about with something a little bit shorter. Some students are tempted to use funny titles or puns. Do not use a funny title unless it is actually funny. Here it might be particularly worthwhile to make sure your friends think the humor comes across before you turn it in. If you plan on trying to publish this paper as a law review note or article someday, you should pay particular attention to the title. Think about what Westlaw or LexisNexis search terms should bring up your paper, and then write your title to make sure that they do.

Publishing

Student-written notes and articles in law reviews have been cited in numerous court opinions, including by the Supreme Court, and have influenced scholarly debate in a variety of ways. While most students publish a note in the law journal they serve as an editor on, every year some students successfully place their papers with outside journals through a competitive process. Publishing an academic paper looks good on your résumé, shares your ideas with the world, and could have an actual impact on the law. If you are going down this road, I strongly recommend Eugene Volokh's book *Academic Legal Writing*.

Before you can publish a paper, you have to write one first. I suggest writing a paper for a class with publication in mind rather than trying to find spare time to write a 25- to 50-page work after class. So sign up for a class with a paper-writing component, or ask a professor to sponsor an independent research project for credit, based on a subject matter that lines up with your writing interest. A professor who has an interest in the area you are writing about may be more interested in sponsoring an independent research project and may provide better feedback, as well as possibly helping you to obtain feedback from other professors. Turning a seminar paper into a note is a great way to maximize your effort. If you are on a specialty journal, you might have to pick a class around the subject matter of your journal—like taking a cyberlaw, intellectual property, or FDA class if you are on a technology journal. Hoping to publish your paper might give you the extra incentive to work harder on it and get an A in the class, even if your paper is never accepted by a journal. If you write something independent of a class, I would still recommend getting feedback from a professor before submitting it to journals.

Journals receive and reject a steady supply of low-quality seminar papers from students; some journals categorically refuse to consider works written by outside students. While your seminar paper provides a great base, you might have to do additional work—heavier citations, a longer introduction, an overall longer paper—to make it worthy of publication. A paper is publishable because of its novelty (it covers a new issue or takes a unique slant on a topic already addressed), writing quality, and timeliness. If you really want to ensure timeliness, come up with a topic based on things you see discussed in the news and pick a seminar that the topic fits. Make sure you paper topic is not preempted by looking on Westlaw or LexisNexis to see what has already been published. If you want to be really cutting-edge, use Google or Google Scholar to search the Web for working drafts of papers that might be forthcoming but are not yet in the legal databases. When publishing a paper, make sure you follow any rules your school might have, such as notifying a professor before the class is over. As a courtesy, you should also notify the professor that you are publishing a former seminar paper and provide a copy of the final published product. If the professor gave you help along the way, be sure to give credit where credit is due. Most authors acknowledge such assistance in their introductory footnote.

If you are trying to publish a paper at one of your school's journals, you'll first have to figure out the process and work through it. If you are not on a journal, or if you are on a specialty journal and your paper covers a topic that is inappropriate for your own journal, other publications at your school might take outside notes. It is likely, of course, that they give preference to papers from their own editors, but they might take proposed notes as a part of a write-on process, an open competition, or something less formal, so ask the editor-in-chief or whoever coordinates note submissions. Several competitions also exist that publish law student papers, some of which even include a cash prize. These are discussed more thoroughly in Chapter 12.

It will likely be more difficult to place a paper with a journal at another law school. There are two specific advantages, though, to publishing externally. First, because you went through a competitive submission process, rather than merely having your note published by your journal because you are on the editorial board, it is at least slightly more prestigious and looks better on your résumé. Of course, if there is a great disparity between the quality of journals and quality of schools, such as if you are on the board of the *Michigan Law Review* and a secondary specialty journal at the University of Wyoming is willing to publish your piece, the *Michigan Law Review* probably looks better. Second, an outside journal might publish your paper as an article rather than as a note, which often looks more prestigious. Many journals do not accept submissions from students at other law schools, but some do.

After Professor Eugene Volokh encouraged students at a conference I attended to submit notes to other schools, I put extra effort into the seminar paper I was working on, polished it, and submitted it to a handful of technology- and media-focused journals. Several weeks later I received two offers to publish the paper as an article. I know other students who've enjoyed similar success, publishing as an article in a lower-ranked secondary journal, and I have heard of some very bright students placing papers in much more prestigious law reviews. If you are going to try to place your paper with an outside journal, here is how the process works.

The Submission Process

To understand how law reviews work, try to think about the students who serve as submissions editors. A small number of law journals are peer-reviewed, but most are run by 3Ls. Law students really like heavily footnoted papers because editors know how to check footnotes and can probably spot errors in footnotes and citations more easily than errors in your analysis or an unsound proposal. Make sure your footnotes and citations sufficiently conform to *Bluebook* rules to get past the submissions editors. There is a submission cycle for law reviews that flows around the submissions editors' schedules. The peak time comes after new editorial boards take over a journal but before the exam season starts (February to April). Then things slow down as exams and summer jobs get in the way. The secondary submission season starts up again in August, when students return from summer jobs, and eases to a halt when the fall semester starts. The traditional advice is to target those time periods, and I think it is a good strategy. With one paper I wrote after law school, though, I decided to break the rules and apply in the late fall. I knew that my law school journal sometimes had a last-minute need for articles while most people were not submitting papers due to authors' leveraging offers, leaving a kind of hole in the process. My coauthor and I ended up having perfect timing—our paper was rejected from numerous journals that were "full" but received some pretty great offers from other journals for publication in the winter or spring issues. Because some journals may be full, you should submit *very* broadly no matter when you submit. There are hundreds of law journals available; target as many as you think is reasonable.

When law review authors receive an offer, the usual custom is to try and leverage it to get an offer from a higher-ranked journal. In other disciplines this conduct would be frowned upon, but it is a big part of the publishing game among lawyers. However, you should not try to leverage an offer from a journal you are a member of to get an offer out of a higher-ranked journal unless you are completely sure that your journal accepts such behavior; otherwise you are acting in bad taste. When you receive an offer from a journal, you will want to get the details of it right away— when the deadline is for you to accept the offer and whether they are offering to publish it as an article or a note. Then contact other journals and ask them to "expedite" their review of your paper, telling them which journal you received an offer from and your deadline for responding to it. At journals that receive a large number of submissions, this may be the only way that your article gets looked at in a timely manner.

Essentially, law reviews are much more likely to look at your paper once some other law review has accepted it and implicitly guaranteed its quality. Because the *Harvard Law Review* probably will not be impressed if a very low-ranked law review makes an offer, authors usually employ expedite requests in waves, trying to get the next group of journals to make an offer with a new deadline and then requesting an expedited review from journals ranked slightly higher than that one. If you are lucky enough to get an offer and are trying to figure out which journals to expedite, or if you have multiple offers and want to decide which one to accept, there are two common approaches. One is to look at the Washington and Lee University law journal rankings (*http://lawlib.wlu.edu/lj/*); the other is to simply look at a school's *U.S. News and World Report* ranking, since publishing with a top-100 law school's journal is more prestigious than publishing with a tier-four journal. This becomes complicated with the proliferation of secondary specialty journals, which are particularly likely to accept student submissions. Washington and Lee's rankings, while not without their own problems, provide a way to compare journals within a specialty, but it is still helpful to compare the schools where the journals are located. It is also considered more prestigious to publish in a print journal than in an online-only one, even though people mostly read the print articles online.

The submissions process is very simple if you are willing to pay for it. The ExpressO (*http://law.bepress.com/expresso/*) system makes law review submissions quick and easy, delivering papers to more than 500 journals and all of the top-100 ones. It also costs $2 for every journal you submit to. Some schools, probably mostly the top law schools, will pay for their students' submissions and/or permit them to use the school's administrative account directly to send the submissions. The University of Michigan reimbursed me for $50 worth of submissions. E-mail your dean of students to find out if your school will cover it. Even if ExpressO's cost is out of your reach, it is still worth signing up for. New account users receive one free delivery, which is helpful because a few journals only take submissions through ExpressO. ExpressO also has a list of which journals are full and not accepting new submissions, including when they will start taking new ones, and it notes which journals are officially not open to submissions from law students. A variety of free options are also available for reaching law journals.

Washington and Lee University has started a Web site called LexOpus (*http://lexopus.yiil.org/lexopus/*), designed to create temporarily exclusive offers to law journals. They boast of having almost 500 journals accepting submissions. I had no success using their site and privately heard from editors who complained about the system. I would approach it with great skepticism unless it becomes more widely accepted. The Social Science Research Network (SSRN; *http://www.ssrn.com*) has a submissions system as well, but it has fewer journals and limits your free submissions to only twenty per paper. During law school I was skeptical about whether the system worked, but I later placed a paper at a top-100 law journal through it, so it works to some extent.

The simplest way to submit is to send a plain old e-mail to the journal's submission address. Washington and Lee (*http://lawlib.wlu.edu/lj/*) maintains a list of submission addresses and journal Web sites (which sometimes have a submission form but usually provide an address for e-mail submissions). Northern Kentucky University (*http://chaselaw.nku.edu/faculty/ejournals.php*) has a great system that allows you to check the law reviews you want to submit a paper to and creates a list that you can copy and paste into your e-mail. The Web site's coverage is not complete, but it is a great tool. The least expensive way to reach a lot of journals might be to use some combination of all of the above.

If you fail to place a paper, do not give up. You might be able to resubmit it in another submission cycle or after law school, when more journals will be open to hearing from you. One student I know could not place his manuscript with a law journal but received an offer from one of the Federalist Society's publications. He felt disappointed that the piece would not be available on Westlaw or LexisNexis, but his ideas are still out there, and he has another line on his résumé to be proud of. You can also shorten a piece and try to publish it in a bar journal. Some state bars (such as Colorado) publish a single journal, but others (such as Michigan) have numerous journals for their various sections, including specialty publications on tax law, environmental law, local governments, and employment law. These typically publish much shorter pieces with fewer footnotes and are more likely to be open to students. You will have to look at your state bar's Web site to see what is out there and read some articles in the publications to see what their styles are like. If you can boil your idea down to plain English in a short, citation-free format (something like 500–750 words), you could also create an op-ed out of the manuscript and try to place it in newspapers.

What to Include with the Paper

Your submission should include more than just the manuscript. Almost all journals want a *curriculum vitae* (CV) or résumé. This one should have an academic focus, highlighting anything that makes you look smart or prestigious, particularly anything you have published in the past or in other disciplines. Do not try to hide the fact that you are a student; the editors will find out eventually, and all you will manage to do by obscuring that fact is hurt your credibility. You will also need to prepare a cover letter, which is one of the most important parts of getting your paper read. Your cover letter should explain what the paper is about, its general thesis, and what makes it special, novel, or original. In other words, it shows why the paper matters. The cover letter should sell both the paper and you. If you have prior work or publications that sound good, emphasize them. Keep it to a page or less and keep your language clear. Professor Volokh provides sample cover letters in his book *Academic Legal Writing*. You can also find free sample cover letters and some advice on drafting cover letters on the Concurring Opinions blog (*http://www.concurringopinions.com/archives/2009/08/sample-law-review-submission-cover-letters.html*).

Most authors also prepare an abstract, a short summary of the paper, which you absolutely must do if you are posting and submitting over SSRN. An abstract is designed to give your readers a sufficiently good first impression that they want to read the paper. An abstract should be 250-400 words, cover the general thesis of your paper, make clear what is original about your paper, and be error-free. Put some real time into this, as it might be the first thing a reader comes across, and try to get feedback from friends or professors on it. If you are unsure of what an abstract should look like, examine some other papers on SSRN.

Promoting Your Paper

The most common way of promoting a paper is posting it on SSRN's Legal Scholarship Network (*http://www.ssrn.com/lsn/index.html*). This makes it available to a broader community that might not have access to paid Web sites. SSRN distributes abstracts and links to new papers to its members (mostly law professors) over e-mail. Posting a paper after acceptance but before publication can also generate helpful feedback from the academic community and help you to fix errors before it is printed. Watch the terms of your publishing agreement, though. Most journals are willing to let you post a paper on SSRN after it is published, but some will not let you post or distribute an advance draft. Professor Volokh suggests promoting a paper by sending copies to individuals you cite and prominent professors in the field. Any way you can get people to notice it—linking to it on Facebook, blogging or tweeting about it, or sending it to law blogs that cover its subject matter—might be worth doing. You can also use op-eds to promote a paper after it is accepted for publication or after it is printed. After you've spent all this time writing, editing, submitting, leveraging, and re-editing the paper, you should put in some more work to make sure people actually read your ideas.

Key Points

- Watch for possible paper topics in issues you encounter during summer internships or other out-of-classroom legal experiences.
- A circuit split is a classic idea for a paper topic.
- Since professors are legal scholars, it is usually a good idea to ask them for topic ideas and feedback on your writing. Be sure to credit them in your paper if they give you advice or input, and send them a copy of the work if you end up publishing it.
- Check out legal blogs for ways to look at topics or for topic ideas.
- A good topic is essential to a good paper.
- Learn to use WestLaw and LexisNexis efficiently.
- Google your topic to find information not in the popular legal databases.
- Avoid being overly wordy in your writing.
- Write the analysis section first, then the intro and conclusion.
- Solve the problem. Don't simply analyze an article, explain the law, or identify the problem without providing a solution.
- Edit! Edit! Edit some more!
- If you can, try to write class papers that can also be submitted to law reviews for publication.
- If a journal makes an offer to publish your article, you can leverage the offer to get it published in a higher-ranked journal, which is more prestigious.

Chapter 12

Winning Scholarships, Awards, Fellowships, and Grants

Law school is expensive. If you are like most law students, you are probably worried about how much law school costs and whether or not you will be able to pay back the loans you are taking out to finance school. There are lots of grants, fellowships, and scholarships available to law students to offset the cost of law school. Even if you are blessed enough to have a full scholarship, most external scholarship checks are made payable to you and can go toward your cost of living. First you need to find the scholarships. These scholarships can be either internal (from your law school) or external (from outside organizations). Internal scholarships usually are awarded before you even start attending law school, based on set criteria, and are discussed briefly at the end of this chapter. This chapter focuses primarily on winning outside scholarships.

Outside scholarships fall into two primary categories: those based on who you are, and those based on what you will do for the scholarship. The "who-you-are" scholarships require less writing in your application and are based on set criteria that you either do or do not already meet. These are traditional scholarships. The other category consists primarily of writing contests (some of which require in-depth scholarship papers) but also include fellowships and grants to support specific projects. To win the money available through outside scholarships, you must know what scholarships are available, know yourself and the kind of background and skills

145

you can bring to the scholarship hunt, know what it takes to win a particular scholarship, and plan your strategy based on these things.

To start finding scholarship money, begin collecting and saving information on the available scholarships. Your law school is almost certainly already collecting this information, even if they are doing a poor job of communicating it to you. The scholarship contests are sending advertisements to your school's financial aid department. Find out how your law school distributes information about scholarships. Some schools maintain a page on their financial aid Web site, some send out e-mail on a regular schedule, some physically post information on scholarships in or near their office, and some maintain a physical book of available scholarships. Once you have found out how your school keeps and distributes this information, check it and check back later as new opportunities may come in. Most law students do not pay attention to these scholarship opportunities, even when their schools make a habit of regularly distributing information about them via spam e-mails.

I am not sure why most students do not pay attention to the outside scholarship opportunities that their schools collect. Many financial aid offices fail to promote these scholarships, and those that do often notify students either too far in advance of a deadline to make applying practical or too close to the deadline for a student to successfully apply. But I think most students are so overwhelmed by law school that the additional work of applying for outside scholarship money crushes their interest. But managing your workload and being strategic in your approach to outside scholarships will keep the work from overwhelming you.

A thorough search for outside scholarship money will involve going beyond your own law school and require at least some Internet research, but you can still let others do most of the work for you. Instead of looking for scholarships directly on organizations' Web sites, I recommend looking at the information other law schools have collected for their students. The University of Idaho has a great directory of outside scholarships (*http://www.law.uidaho.edu/external_scholarships*). My own University of Michigan, which also looks at non-law scholarships that law students can apply for, provides all its information on a publicly available Web site (*http://www.law .umich.edu/currentstudents/financialaid/suppres/Pages/default.aspx*). And many schools collect lists of writing competitions with cash prizes, such as *http://law.lclark.edu/ offices/admissions/student_writing_competitions/*.

I doubt that any single school's financial aid office has found all of the scholarships available to law students, but with a little use of Google and by perusing a handful of law school financial aid Web sites, you can see most of what is out there.

Bookmark or store the address of the law school Web sites that you find most helpful in identifying scholarships, and check back at these sites every so often to find new scholarships and watch for new information, particularly this year's deadlines, on scholarships you have already discovered.

■■■ ──────────────────────────── ■■■

Professor Kathryn A. Sampson maintains a blog with posts on legal writing competitions offering cash prizes. On the side of the blog she links to law school Web sites that maintain good listings. *http://legalwritingcompetitions .blogspot.com/*

You must be aware of the deadlines for outside scholarships. Almost all scholarship or writing contest deadlines fall on inconvenient dates. They either occur over summer break when you are distracted by your summer job, in the middle of the semester when you are focused on class and other things, or at the end of the term when you are overwhelmed or exhausted by exams. In your search you may discover a scholarship with a deadline several months away and will have to be deadline-conscious. Or you might find one when the deadline is too close to get an application together. Or you may have narrowly missed this year's deadline and will want to apply next year. Often a contest's deadline for the next year will fall around the same time as this year's deadline. When you have found a contest you are or may be interested in, write its deadline down on your calendar. If the deadline has lapsed, write it down on the same date next year with a note to check for the actual deadline at some point in the future. I loaded appealing scholarship deadlines into my Palm calendar, and it reminded me to apply to a contest the next year that I ended up winning. Be aware of the existence of scholarships and the timeframe to apply, and act on that knowledge when the opportunity comes.

Your Advantage

Before you start your scholarship search, though, you should figure out your personal advantage. First, who are you? Are you a member of a recognized minority group? Specialized scholarships exist for African-American students; lesbian, gay, bisexual, and transgender students; and female students. Beyond traditional minority categories, there are also scholarships for Italian Americans and Irish Americans.

Local bar associations provide scholarships based on the county you went to high school in or the district you plan on practicing in after law school. Ideological groups such as libertarians offer scholarships. Many (highly competitive) public-interest awards are out there. Are you a first-generation college student? Do you have an extreme case of financial need? Are you Jewish, Baptist, or a member of some other organized religion?

As a generic white male who has never performed any meaningful community service—most real community service people do not count being active in politics—I thought these opportunities were for individuals with more interesting backgrounds. But I received scholarships based on where I grew up and my political beliefs.

The second thing to consider in assessing your personal advantage is what you are good at. Do you have good grades? Or an interesting story? Or an impressive résumé? Are you a good writer? Good at writing long or short items? I am great at writing short pieces. My background prior to law school involved writing newspaper columns of about 750 words. My best luck in scholarships came with things that involved shorter writing—general scholarships with short essays or writing contests with low word limits. When I saw writing contests with 50-page limits, I steered away from them. While I have written and published papers that long before, there are others more specialized at that type of writing. Figure out your personal edge and read through the list of scholarships with this in mind.

Successful Applications

Browse the basics of every available scholarship with your personal advantage in mind and keep these scholarships in mind as you work on class assignments. You may be able to develop a paper for a class that fits perfectly with a writing contest. If you are committed to developing the paper for a class, it dramatically increases the likelihood that you will get around to actually submitting your entry. This principle is less helpful for scholarships other than writing contests. With these contests, perseverance can be more important.

Even if you apply for a scholarship and fail, apply again the next year if you are still eligible for the scholarship. As a 1L, I applied for a scholarship from the Institute for Humane Studies and was shot down. The next year I was awarded $6000. As a 2L, I applied to the Federal Bar Association for the Western District of Michigan's scholarship and was shot down. As a 3L, I reapplied and won $1500. When you reapply, learn from your mistakes. The Western District of Michigan scholarship was available to students from the Western District who planned on practicing there. While I was a native of the area, the recent entries on my résumé were all located in the Mountain West. On the second try I went for the throat. I used detailed headings in the essay and included a cover letter that had a bulleted summary to drive home my ties to the Western District:

- I was raised in the Western District.
- I was educated in the Western District.
- I intend to practice in the Western District.
- My entire family lives in the Western District.
- My best friend lives and practices in the Western District.

I made it crystal clear to them that I met the requirements of their scholarship. You should save the files you put together in all of your scholarship applications, as you might be able to use some of them again next year or in other applications. You should also create a special scholarship résumé. This should be longer than your professional résumé and include more detailed entries on the kinds of things that scholarships like (community service, writing, or academics) that you might otherwise treat in a summary fashion for potential employers. If you won some kind of award or scholarship in the past, explain its significance and details on this résumé.

There is a wide variation in the requirements of outside scholarships. Some require a 50-page paper while others require only a 250-word statement plus a résumé. Some require letters of recommendation from professors. Some require short essays and a more substantial writing sample that could have been used elsewhere. Some contests offer thousands of dollars (and usually require more work in the application), and others offer a mere travel scholarship to an ABA contest (and simply require a statement of interest). Some basic lessons apply to all of these contests.

Always proofread your application, essays, résumé, and any supporting documents. Proofreading your scholarship entries is extremely important. It may seem obvious, but you can easily get caught up in law school and the other things in life and either find yourself too busy to proofread and revise or too distracted to proofread accurately. When I was turned down for a fellowship, I assumed that it was because the award committee was either biased against people like me or foolish in failing to see the diamond in the rough. Then, for some reason, the year after the rejection I looked at the computer file of my application and noticed that it was full of obvious, stupid, glaring, and shocking errors. I had written the application while under the strain of first-year exams. Had I taken 15 minutes to catch my breath and proofread the application, I might have won.

You do not have to have a sure chance of winning to justify applying. I have been rejected from more law school scholarships than I have won. Some I applied to more than once and was rejected each time. But I have won more than $10,000 in outside scholarships and earned a pretty good rate of return on my time spent applying. Once you've won a scholarship, your rate of return will increase when you apply to other programs.

Scholarships and awards have an almost "chicken-and-the-egg" problem. Once you've won an award, your résumé looks more prestigious, and winning other awards is easier. If you win anything, update your résumé and apply for more. Finally, let any faculty who write you letters of recommendation know if you win an award they recommended you for, and thank them regardless of the outcome. Always follow up with your professors to build stronger relationships.

Writing Contests

The first rule of winning writing contests is to consult with others if allowed. For example, have your friends look over your essays. Thank your friends for their feedback in the first footnote of your essays in the style that law professors use, just to be clear that you did have some outside input. As a general rule, writing contests that require papers that are more like law review articles will allow outside input on your paper. Contests that do not allow outside comments will probably say so clearly in the rules.

Carefully read the rules of the contest before you start writing. Watch for limits on the topic, page length, and footnotes. Pay special attention to any discussion of the grading criteria. Write your paper, or edit a paper that's already written, to meet the criteria for winning. After finishing your paper, check the rules one last time to make sure you've complied. There is no reason to send in a paper that will be rejected on some technicality. And there is no reason to send in a paper that has obvious errors in grammar, clarity, or reasoning, which is why you want your friends to look over your paper.

Before having friends read over and proofread or edit your work, talk about the topic and your thesis with them. Explain what you plan on writing about and see what kind of questions they ask or counterarguments they bring up. These kind of intellectual exercises lead to good scholarly legal writing; it's what your professors do in preparing their law review articles. Whenever possible, you should get input from a professor on your contest entry. Your professors are excellent writers. Most legal academics are hired based on their scholarship, which means they publish law review articles. For a legal writing contest, you are doing a junior version of the same thing that your law professors excel at. A professor who has knowledge of the subject area of your contest may be able to help suggest topics or refine your ideas, but all of your professors will probably have advice on how to write a better entry. Again, if you win a contest where a professor helped, follow up and let the professor know how it turned out. This will help build your relationship with that professor.

Working Fellowships

Another opportunity to gain extra money comes through working fellowships. These programs usually require you to enter a competitive application process and, after receiving the cash award, perform some kind of work project that the funders support. Examples include working on certain clinic projects, researching planning and urban development, and working on scholarly activities that promote free markets and religion. When considering applying to a fellowship, you should think about the work you'll do after receiving the award, not just the work involved in putting together the application. These fellowships are different from regular jobs because you are funded to work on a project, usually with only a report at the end. The stipend may also be taxed differently than a job would. There are fewer of these fellowships than any of the opportunities I covered previously, but they are worth investigating further if you come across any during your research that match your interests. I won a $1250 fellowship to support scholarly research from an organization that funds graduate students in general, not typically law students. This money came at a very helpful time and I enjoyed working on the project.

Deciding Which Contests to Pursue

After you have done your research, you will be shocked at how many opportunities law students have to get money from outside organizations. There are too many scholarship programs for you to apply to them all, and writing contests take too much time to apply to more than a handful, if any. I have a simple set of rules, or calculations, to decide whether to undertake the work to apply to a particular opportunity. Here is my approach.

Start by asking yourself how many students you think are likely to apply. You will not know the hard numbers, so this isn't an opportunity to develop an actual game-theory model, but simply thinking this through will help you make a strategic choice. Ask yourself who can apply to any given contest. Is it limited by location, age, gender, or school? How much money is involved? How much work is required to complete an entry? When is the deadline, and how much advance notice did students have of the deadline? How specialized or odd is the contest? Basically, a contest whose workload is easy, whose criteria limit the kind of students that can apply, and whose prize money is high will attract a lot of attention. A contest with little advanced notice, an unrealistic deadline, and an odd or specialized topic will have fewer applicants.

Next, realistically consider just how well you meet the criteria the contest is judged on. Do you write well? Do you write this kind of thing well? Consider the factors we discussed earlier. Then try to figure out how much *extra* time it will take to apply to this contest. If you are applying to a scholarship that requires a short personal statement relevant to the contest, a statement of your career and professional goals, and a résumé, this will take very little time if you have already written a short essay on your career goals and prepared a scholarship-focused résumé. Similarly, if you wrote a paper on an antitrust law topic for a class, polishing it up to enter it in a writing contest on antitrust law will not take nearly as much work as writing a paper from scratch for a writing contest on labor law.

Finally, examine the payout for the contest. Are there any other things of value you could win in addition to the money, such as travel to a conference to receive the award, publication of your paper (a great résumé booster), or a plaque? What value do any of these things have to you? I had an interest in an academic career, so things that sounded scholarly or offered the chance for publication had extra value to me. If you want to work for a regional firm's bankruptcy practice group in Cleveland but come from a less-than-stellar law school, winning a contest from the bankruptcy section of the Federal Bar Association for the Northern District of Ohio may have extra value to you.

Putting this all together will show you what contests are worth your time. The number of applications and how well you meet the criteria of those contests will help you figure out your chance of winning. Your chance of winning times the value of the payout should be greater than the cost divided by the extra time it will take to apply. Of course, this is not a real mathematical equation, since you know only your information and nothing about the other contestants, but this mental exercise is the kind of strategic thinking necessary for law school decisions.

Formula for Evaluating Contest Opportunities

Chance of Winning $\times$ Payout > Cost/Extra Time to Apply

Internal Scholarships

It seems that law students receive much more money from their own law schools than from external scholarships. These can be merit-based, need-based, or both. Scholarship decisions are usually made during the admissions process, though some schools also reward those who earn high grades their first year with enhanced scholarships. Also, if your financial need status changes significantly, be sure to inform your law school's financial aid office. The only other piece of advice I can offer in dealing with your school is to consider bargaining with them when you have the ability to make a credible threat of picking another school.

During the admissions process you can actually try to respond to whatever financial aid offer you receive by asking for more. Some schools are more likely to bargain with you than others, but as a basic rule, if you have something they want (e.g., an LSAT score higher than their current average, which would help their *U.S. News and World Report* rankings), your potential law school may up the offer to secure your attendance. It's an awkward thing to ask someone for more money, but I was able to negotiate a bigger scholarship by leveraging one school's offer against another.

Another opportunity could open up at the end of your first year if you earn excellent grades and have the opportunity to transfer to another law school (see Chapter 8). It is possible, though difficult, to convince a potential transfer school to give you a merit-based scholarship. Transfer students may still qualify for need-based scholarships, including potentially large ones. One student I know earned high-enough grades to transfer out and convinced her law school administration to give her a full scholarship. You are unlikely to go from no aid to a full scholarship based on your bargaining skills alone, but given the success others have had, you should try.

Key Points
Types of Scholarships
- Internal
- External
- Writing contests
- Financial need
- Merit
- Community service
- Special interest and minority
- Fellowships and grants

General Steps to Winning Scholarships
- Research and explore information on scholarships according to your abilities, inclinations, talents, and eligibility.
- Write down deadlines, and check back for new submission dates for yearly contests if this year's deadline has passed.
- Draft your application or essay.
- Proofread, and have others give you input and review your materials if the rules allow.
- Thank those who helped you in writing your essay, with special acknowledgement to professors.
- Apply before the deadline.
- Do not give up; the more you apply, the greater your chances of success.
- If you win, update your résumé to reflect your achievement.

Chapter 13

Working in Law School

As most of us choose to go to law school because of the job we hope to get after it, this chapter focuses on the career-related decisions and experiences you face during law school. Many students find the job hunt to be just as stressful as their exams. With some understanding of the process, you might find it less daunting. At the very least, knowing the work you face in looking for work can help you balance other time priorities. This and the next four chapters are designed to make that process a little easier.

For most students, law school is a full-time job and then some. Some students, myself included, work part-time jobs while in law school for the extra money, the experience, or because they are simply uncomfortable with not having a job. Before discussing the advantages and disadvantages of working part-time in law school, I will discuss a decision you have to make before school: whether to take on work full-time and school part-time.

Full-Time Worker, Part-Time Student

A number of law schools offer distinct part-time programs, often with classes at night, and on rare occasion, a school without a distinct program might accommodate a special student with a part-time track. Some students take part-time programs because the pace is more convenient or fits around family obligations, but the greatest appeal of such programs is the ability to work. Before undertaking this dual life, potential students should realize that, while it is absolutely doable, it's very difficult.

You have to go into it knowing that your social life outside of work is school and your social life outside school is work. You will have very little time to do any activities other than work or school, and your schedule will force you to become very efficient—like learning to study flash cards while waiting at the airport during travel for work. If you work a nine-to-five job, you'll spend your evenings and weekends studying. At many programs, full-time is 14-15 credits and part-time is 11 credits, which means you are doing 40 hours of work for only one fewer class. Outside of the possibility of personal misery, there are other downsides.

If you are in a night program whose classes are open to full-time students as well, you might find yourself at a disadvantage in having less time for exam prep compared to the peers you are graded against. As a full-time worker, you might miss out on the law school life. Even if your school is welcoming to part-time students, your busy schedule might preclude you from being involved in student organizations or connecting with your peers on a social basis.

You might miss out on networking opportunities that would otherwise benefit your career in the long run. These opportunities are more likely to be available to part-time students in better-established part-time programs, but even then your schedule and energy might prevent you from taking full advantage of them. Your part-time status also might prevent you from transferring schools (which a few students do at the end of their 1L year) as some (but not all) higher-ranked schools are less welcoming to former part-timers, and your combination of credits could mean you have too few to transfer at the end of your 1L year and too many at the end of your 2L year.

You also miss out on the chance to gain legal experience. Legal experience, as I'll discuss later in this chapter, is the key to gaining postgraduation employment. The big law firms hire summer associates with the expectation that they will fill their future ranks of attorneys from this pool. Your full-time day job will keep you busy during the day and, if it's a year-round job, might not offer much of a summer break. It's possible to get around this by doing a part-time externship for credit instead of taking classes for one semester, which at least one law school requires, but it is not the same thing as a full-time summer associate position.

You could also plan to participate in the on-campus interview process, try to land a "biglaw" summer associate position for the semester before your final year (likely your 4L year as a part-time student), and if you do land one, quit your job to start at the firm. Students have actually done this, but after the summer, you face going through your final year of law school without drawing a salary, which can present problems if you are not prepared.

You also face the opportunity cost of lost legal wages by delaying your graduation. If you expect to earn substantially more after graduation than you earned before going to law school, delaying those big earnings for a year or two is itself a cost. But a legal education is not a guarantee of higher wages, and you should consider the average starting salary of your law school's alums. The wage gap between your day job and your post–law school job tends to reflect the different starting salaries found between graduates of a top national school and a local one. The financial question can be more complicated than it appears on the surface.

The obvious upside to working while you're in law school is that you earn more money. You know the wages you'll lose by giving up your job, but other costs are harder to see. Of course there's health insurance, but you should also think about the money that won't be put into your 401(k) and the loss of things like seniority and vacation days. If you think you'd go back to the same company after law school, this is a particular advantage to working. If you have a professional job, working full-time could also benefit you in an odd way by lowering people's expectations of your GPA. If you maintain a decent GPA during law school while working an impressive job, potential employers may favor you over students with similar GPAs but tons of free time.

If you're going to work full-time, you must find ways to balance your work and school. Both your school and your work believe they are entitled to be your number-one priority. Seeking out a program that offers support for part-time students (including evening or weekend classes) is important. You need professors who will understand that you have commitments outside of law school, and those in part-time programs should be at least slightly more tolerant. If possible, try to sell your employer on your legal education. Before starting law school, explain how the law degree will help you do your day job and help the company, then follow up by talking about how classes are helping you perform your everyday duties.

One student I know pulled this off successfully. One key to her success was saving up her vacation days and using them around finals or big papers in her legal writing class. This study time was huge, as she found that even a couple days of solid studying helped her to catch up. This student decided to make the switch from part-time to full-time law school after two years, which allowed her to wrap law school up in four rather than five years. She enjoyed being a full-time law student much more than being a full-time worker and part-time student.

Full-Time Student, Part-Time Worker

Law school can be overwhelming. You shouldn't feel pressured to work a part-time job just because other students do. Many students simply have no business working. But for those with extra time on their hands or in need of money, part-time work may be the answer.

As with all things in law school, make sure you work for the right reasons. One friend of mine worked a few stray shifts for his previous employer for no good reason—the job offered no helpful experience and he didn't need the money. He did it just because he was asked. I worked in law school mostly because I wanted to keep earning at least some money. Having worked as an undergrad, it felt too strange to be income-free. During my 1L year I worked miscellaneous projects using skills I acquired before law school. As a 1L, I had no skills to apply to any kind of legal work. I did some consulting for my previous employer, wrote newspaper columns and book summaries, and did a little bit of political consulting. I enjoyed having the income, but working during your 1L year is generally not worth it. My 1L jobs were all continuations of things I was doing prior to law school.

If you are hoping to find work during your 1L year, the best strategy may be to try to make arrangements with your existing employer or networks before starting law school. Law schools generally discourage, prohibit, or restrict employment for 1Ls in various ways, though, so be aware of this road block. Some law schools hire students for non-law jobs, such as staffing the front desk at the library or mailing out things in admissions. These generally pay very little. If you need the money, they might be worth it, but I would suggest looking for jobs that add some relevant legal experience after your 1L year.

Working during your 2L or 3L year is much more common and easier to arrange. Some law schools hire students with decent grades as faculty research assistants or in some kind of tutoring role. While tutoring or academic support positions don't let you develop actual legal experience, they still help you demonstrate your mastery of a particular subject and look better on a résumé than a job contacting admitted students and asking them to pay a deposit. Tutoring can also be fun. I spent a semester during my 3L year tutoring students in torts and constitutional law as a way to jog my memory and better prepare myself for the bar. I thoroughly enjoyed getting to know the 1Ls and helping them adjust to law school.

Most research assistants work directly for a specific professor and are hired by that professor. Some schools also have general faculty research assistants who work in the library on whatever task a professor needs and are hired directly by the library. As with academic support positions, research assistant jobs pay very little. The hours, though, tend to be light, and professors are good at working around your exam schedule. Being a research assistant helps you hone your research skills, gives you a taste of the kind of work academics do, lets you build a relationship with a faculty member that can generate a great letter of recommendation, and looks good on your résumé. I liked working as a research assistant for a professor who was working on an election law paper. She was even kind enough to thank me in the published version.

Professors end up hiring research assistants in a variety of different ways. They might announce the opening on the school's job bulletin or internal system, they might tell their class, or they might approach a specific student. Ask around, or approach someone in career services, to find out how these positions are filled at your school. If your law school is a part of a bigger university, attorneys teaching in other departments—the business school, for example—might hire law students as their research assistants. Similarly, your university might have a legal department that takes school-semester law clerks. I worked for the University of Michigan Health System Legal Office for a semester. The experience wasn't particularly valuable, but it looked nice on my résumé.

A variety of law firms hire students during the academic year. I would suggest looking at smaller, local firms in the area near your law school. The hiring patterns vary more than the summer-associate hiring discussed later in this chapter, so the best way to find these openings may be to look on your school's jobs bulletin board, talk to career services, and even chat with staff at the local bar association. These local firms may hire students because they need people to perform the work, not as a part of a broader recruiting strategy the way some firms hire summer associates. If you spent your summer working for a law firm, it might be easier to approach them about doing work for them doing the school year. This is much more common among small firms but not entirely unheard of among larger ones. Your pay and experience working at a law firm during the academic year can be much better than some of the law school jobs.

I managed to land a job working at a law firm 1500 miles away from my school during my 3L year. I found a posting on my school's career services Web site from a law firm looking to hire a bright student to telecommute—work remotely via e-mail and overnight mail—on writing briefs and motions. I originally applied to the job as 2L but never heard back. I reapplied as a 3L and landed one of the best jobs I've ever had. I was paid well, was able to set my own hours and work around my exam schedule, and did meaningful work that gave me great experience, all because I was willing to take a chance on an odd-sounding job.

If you're more concerned about the experience than with the money, then unpaid externships might be best. Prosecutors, public defenders, and judges often take school-year externs. Working for a prosecutor or public defender can give you great experience, and few things are more prestigious than working for a highly regarded judge. These positions can also open doors. An attorney I know was hired after graduation into the prosecutor's office where he had worked full-time during the summer and part-time during the school year. One of the externs from a local law school was hired into a prestigious postgraduation judicial clerkship—one normally limited to graduates of top-ten law schools—because she was an extern for the judge. Generally, you can also earn class credit at your law school for working in these unpaid externships.

Most attorneys are mindful of your exam schedule and willing to work around it. Working for nonattorneys in jobs outside of the legal field could present a different set of difficulties. I found working while in law school to be helpful and fulfilling, but I wouldn't recommend it to anyone who feels overwhelmed by the daily grind. Many students (probably most) do not work at all during law school and have historically ended up perfectly fine, although that could be changing.

Key Points

Full-time Worker, Part-Time Student

- Some law schools have part-time programs.
- This situation can be hard to balance, and all time outside of work will be dedicated to schoolwork, with little to no time for socialization.
- Consider issues such as employer and school support, expectations for wages after law school, and lack of time for participation in things like student organizations.
- Working full-time in an impressive job may lower a future potential employer's expectations of your GPA, so that they may potentially favor you over a student with a similar GPA who did not work.
- Save up vacation days and use them around finals and deadlines for big papers if your employer permits.

Full-Time Student, Part-Time Worker

- Work for the right reasons.
- Be cognizant that many schools discourage, prohibit, or restrict employment for 1Ls.
- As a 1L student, you will probably find more success securing part-time employment if you contact your employer before law school.
- Tutoring or academic-support positions demonstrate mastery of a subject and look good on a résumé.
- Overall, aim to work at a job that adds relevant legal experience.
- The 2L and 3L years are easier ones in which to get a job.
- Working as a research assistant for a professor can provide a valuable networking connection with that professor if you do a good job.
- One source of employment is your school's legal department. Some law firms, especially smaller local firms, might have some interest in hiring a student for light work during the school year.
- Unpaid externships in a prosecutor's, public defender's, or judge's office offer a decent chance at securing legal experience during the school year.

Chapter 14

THE 1L JOB SEARCH

THE SEARCH FOR A JOB FOR THE SUMMER FOLLOWING YOUR 1L YEAR is arguably the most difficult one you will face in law school because there are fewer jobs for 1Ls and you have fewer skills to offer potential employers. The 1L job search matters because it helps you land a job for the summer after your 2L year, which generally feeds into full-time employment after law school. Your 1L job can also set you up for a part-time job during school and improve your application if you try to transfer law schools. Your goals are to land a job someplace where law is practiced, develop a writing sample at that job, and end up with something interesting to talk about with prospective employers during your 2L interviews. The job search process can be frustrating and time-consuming, but it is important to invest the necessary time. Meanwhile, you still have to keep up your studies and cannot neglect your grades. This is yet another area in law school where striking a balance is critical.

***

Timeline

From day one: Attend events and network.

November: Prepare documents, research employers, start a spreadsheet, and meet with career services.

December: Apply for jobs at big firms and under big judges. Visit people over Christmas break.

January-February: Send out more applications targeting midsize employers and follow up on earlier applications.

March-April: Send out more applications targeting smaller employers and follow up on earlier applications.

Be patient, brace yourself for rejections and delays, and keep trying even if your first applications do not work out. Attending a lower-ranked school often makes finding a 1L summer job more difficult but nowhere near impossible. It might keep you from landing a job at a big firm, but very few students at top law schools manage to land one of these for their first summer. A less prestigious school might make it more difficult to land a job in a region that neither you nor your school has any ties to, though. If you are worried about your school's *U.S. News and World Report* ranking affecting your job search, let that motivate you to apply more broadly and work harder at the search process—do not give up.

My initial advice is to take advantage of your school's career services office, but also recognize its limits. Career services counselors at some schools see so many students that their thinking risks becoming mechanical. If you are not at a national school, they might put a disproportionate amount of their effort into helping a few superstars. Your career services staff simply might not be all that good. But they might be great, so start your process by going to them and seeing what help they have to offer. Every career services office should be able to help with your résumé and point you to a list of summer jobs. Great career service offices can do a lot more. However, the National Association for Law Placement (NALP) Principles and Standards, a set of guidelines for ethical law-student recruiting that most law schools abide by, prevent career services from meeting with 1Ls until November 1 to keep you from jumping into the job search too early. You can prepare for your meeting with career services before this date, though.

Résumés and Cover Letters

To start your job search process, put together a good legal-focused résumé. Emphasize your law-related skills. Potential employers recognize that first-years do not have relevant legal experience on their résumés. That makes it hard for all 1Ls to land a job, but it does not mean that all will be left without prospects.

Try to keep your résumé in chronological order and highlight your accomplishments with bullet points under the name of the job or school where you accomplished them. Do not include an "objective" section—the obvious objective here is to get your first legal experience. After this you will always have an objective section. But try to find a way now to highlight the skills in your past jobs that line up with the kind of things lawyers do. For example, you can emphasize how you used research and writing skills at a past job working for the legislature or how you gained experience serving and interacting with clients at a sales job. In all cases, your résumé should be without errors and entirely professional (do not list an e-mail address like princess4eva@yahoo.com when you have a jmiller@yourlawschool.edu address instead).

Most importantly, emphasize your strengths. If you had great work experience prior to law school, push this. If you went straight through college into law school but had impressive grades, load your résumé with your academic honors. If leadership in clubs or your fraternity is the best thing you have to offer, then rely on this. Once you have identified your strengths, eliminate unessential details, including computer skills that everyone has (Word, Westlaw) and that you have references available upon request. Given how many résumés prospective employers receive and how little time they have to review them, you do not want to include any distractions. Ask your career services office to look over the résumé, and get input from any friends or family members who have good professional instincts. Start this process early in the year so you do not have to worry about it around exam time and will be able to meet any deadlines you encounter later.

You might need to develop more than one résumé based on the employer or the employer's location. For example, judges often tend to like to learn about the human side of applicants and often expect personal information (e.g., hobbies and activities) on résumés; law firms might not. You might tailor a résumé to promote your ties to a specific city or region to demonstrate to an employer why exactly you want to be there (if your permanent residence is in Denver, put both your law school address and your permanent address on the top of résumés going to Denver). And make sure the name of your résumé file has your name in it and nothing else—"Jason_Miller_Resume.doc," not "summer res.doc" or "Jason_Miller_Nonprofit_Resume.doc." Much of your customization should come in your cover letters.

In today's legal job market, generic cover letters are insufficient. As you research law firms and government agencies, your cover letters should reflect what you learn about them. Explain why you want to work there in particular—why your interests or background line up with what they do. And be sure to address employers individually and correctly. Your cover letter should also address your ties to the region, except when those ties are so obvious that an explanation is unnecessary.

Before you write the letter, identify the most persuasive reasons the employer should hire you, which reasons you need to emphasize or explain, and how the job fits with your goals. Then write it, starting with a brief opening paragraph that identifies who you are and what you are applying for (as well as any personal or geographic connections to the employer). Then discuss your qualifications, highlighting items from your résumé that match the requirements of the job, and next connect this information into a convincing pitch to hire you. Finally, conclude with something standard such as, "Please contact me if you would like any additional information." At all costs, keep your cover letter to one page.

Research

Researching potential employers can take a while. But the more potential jobs you find and apply to, the better your chances of finding one. To use your time more efficiently, I recommend putting together a spreadsheet to track the employer, the employer's location, the employer's contact information, any details you might need for a cover letter (e.g., practice areas or points of interest), and when you applied. It is important to apply to jobs beyond your dream position, which means applying to any place you are willing to go. You are most likely to be successful at finding a job in a region you have some ties to. Accordingly, you should focus on places where you have lived, your parents live, your siblings live, your spouse grew up, or any place you can make some compelling claim to have an interest in. Local ties indicate that you will come back in the future and the investment in you is not wasted. It is a better use of your time to focus your research and work on specific areas than to throw generic applications all over the place.

Start your research by taking advantage of your school's job listings, and if you can find a way to access listings at other schools, use those too. These listings reflect only a small number of the possible jobs, and your peers are also focusing on them, so independent research is important. Web sites such as the NALP Directory of Legal Employers (*www.nalpdirectory.com*) and Martindale-Hubbell (*www.martin dale.com*) contain lists of law firms. Most of the summer jobs at big law firms go to 2Ls, and many law firms only hire 2Ls. The few big firms that hire 1Ls schedule on-campus interviews at higher-ranked schools, usually early in the second semester after grades come out. Few 1Ls find success through these programs, though, and the ones who do often end up with a big-firm job in their hometown for that first summer. One top school points out that its winter interview program exists only to "supplement, not supplant" the rest of the 1L job search. While these big-firm jobs are hard for 1Ls to get, they do pay very well. Some big firms have special 1L summer clerkship programs for minority students as an attempt to boost diversity at the firm. If you think these programs would be open to you, make a special effort to look into them in the NALP Directory listing for the firm.

Corporations also have in-house legal departments, and some even have satellite offices away from their company headquarters. Many corporations have in-house legal departments, not just Fortune 500 companies, as do big nonprofit entities like hospitals. On the other end of the spectrum, numerous public-interest legal organizations exist to serve the indigent. You might consider volunteering with a local legal-aid organization during the school year to help you identify possible summer positions.

One of the most popular ways for 1Ls to find employment is through government internships. Basically, every state and federal prosecutor and public defender, as well as most judges, take law students as unpaid summer interns. And this can be great experience. Many local prosecutor's offices let law students—sometimes including those who have only completed their first year—go to court. I spent a 1L semester at one of the most clichéd government internships—in a United States Attorney's Office. But as our government has grown to unprecedented levels, so have its legal departments. In Washington, D.C., you have more than just the Department of Justice—the Bureau of Prisons, Equal Employment Opportunity Commission, National Endowment for the Arts, Small Business Administration, and many other organizations employ attorneys. Moreover, many of these agencies have regional offices in various cities. Similarly, state governments employ lawyers in more departments than just the Office of the Attorney General. The Department of Environmental Quality probably employs quite a few lawyers, and the Secretary of State's Office likely has an election law department. And then there are city attorneys—just about any city of over 100,000 people has its own legal department.

Judicial internships—sometimes called externships if done for credit—are an excellent option for 1Ls. They look great on your résumé and offer an inside view into how the system works that future employers find valuable. A bench memo or opinion also makes a great writing sample. The hiring practices of judges likely vary according to their level, federal judges hiring early (perhaps shortly after December 1 or when first-semester grades come back) and state judges hiring later in the season. The smaller the city or lower the level of the court, the more likely you could wait longer before applying, but it probably does not hurt to apply earlier rather than later.

Unfortunately, there is no central database of judicial internships. Similarly, many government agencies that take interns do not even list that they are accepting internship applications. You can check their Web sites, check with your school, or call the office directly to ask what its hiring process is. If you are uncomfortable making the call, you could simply send a résumé addressed to the head of the office (e.g., the county prosecutor or county public defender). You might have to look at state judiciary or county government Web sites to find information on local judges. You can start this research process merely by identifying what possible government agencies and judges are within the areas you want to work.

You might also find opportunities to do legal work at your school. Your professors might hire research assistants over the summer, or your school might hire research assistants to work in the library. While these positions do not give you the practical experience that an internship in a law office does, you still learn legal research and writing skills. If you accept one of these positions, make a particular effort to ensure that your work produces a writing sample.

Finally, tap your network. Think of anyone you know whom you can ask for advice or who might connect you to a summer legal job. Upperclassmen at your school can be a great source; ask them where they spent their 1L summers. Friends at other law schools might help, too. Look at your family members; if none of them are attorneys, are they friends with any? How about your former employers? Even if you did not work in a law office, perhaps your old boss could recommend you to an attorney.

Process and Choices

With 1L summer jobs, as with all things in law, it is important to be aware of deadlines. The NALP Guidelines, which big law firms follow, prohibit firms from accepting résumés before December 1 of your 1L year. A few jobs have deadlines in December, which is a real pain to deal with during exams. I spent my 1L summer at a U.S. attorney's office that had a December application deadline. I walked by a posting near the career services office, noticed the December deadline, and sent my résumé out the same day. I think very few other students applied because of the early deadline, and this helped me to get the position. Even if you have not received your first-semester grades yet, you should still apply for jobs. Employers understand that you might apply for jobs before your grades come back. And while it undoubtedly seems like your professors are taking intolerably long to issue first-semester grades, chances are the same process is playing itself out at other schools, too. Employers know this, and if they want your grades they will ask for them or wait until you update the employer after grades come out.

Even if you do not hear from a firm right away, that does not mean that you were rejected. Sometimes it takes quite a while to hear back. Firms are operating on their own hiring schedules, not yours. Use a follow-up phone call or e-mail if you are unsure. If you do land an interview, it goes without saying that you should dress like a professional. Wear a suit even if the office you are interviewing with has a business-casual dress code. Moreover, dress conservatively even during the after-work and networking events you attend throughout your job-hunting process.

During your 1L summer job search, you should reconcile yourself to the idea of working for free. You work for free during your 1L summer so that you can work for real money later. Future employers do not care whether you were paid or not; they care that you gained experience. Some schools (generally the wealthier national schools) have fellowship programs to fund or subsidize students who work for free at a public-interest organization, so check to see whether your school does this.

It might be helpful to plan on working for free ahead of time, so that you can save some of your student loan money or arrange sublets. If you are broke, I know it sounds harsh for someone to tell you that you should work for free, but you have to gain legal experience so you're not broke in the future. Think of the reason you went to law school—probably to become a lawyer, not to wait tables or work for your mom's business. Gaining summer experience is a part of the process, even if you have to do it for free. The legal hiring market is very competitive, and you do not want to fall a step behind your peers.

If at all possible, take the unpaid legal job over the paid job waiting tables or working construction. If you cannot land a paying legal job and cannot afford to forgo all income, then at least try to find something in the legal field and part-time. More than a few students work evenings and weekends for pay and do legal work during the day. Furthermore, you might be able to split your time (20 hours and 20 hours or 6 weeks and 6 weeks) between an unpaid legal job (such as working for a judge) and a private, paying legal employer. One additional advantage of unpaid work is that you may be able to secure course credit as an externship from your school, although this usually means you will have to pay your school for the privilege of earning the credit.

Summer study-abroad programs are becoming very popular among law students. Some students sign up for a study-abroad program because they could not find summer jobs and studying abroad seems like a productive way to spend the summer. Do not give in to this trap. I know it is hard to put time into applying for jobs while juggling the demands of law school, but you are enrolled in a professional school to try to get a professional job afterward. Should you want to take a trip abroad or a vacation, do so, but do not give up your critical summer work experience. If, on the other hand, you enrolled in law school with no intention of working as an attorney or really are just in it for the experience of broadening your mental horizons, summer study-abroad programs can be great opportunities.

My general advice is to apply broadly to jobs, try to receive a few offers, and then pick from among the offers you actually receive. Deciding which offer is best is a very personal decision. If you are primarily interested in money and have a high-paying offer from one firm and a low-paying offer from another, it is an easy decision. The difficulty comes when you are forced to choose between unpaid offers, between geographic locations, and between a low-prestige paying job and a prestigious unpaid internship. In deciding between unpaid jobs, I tend to advise students to err on the prestigious side. A job at the United States Attorney's Office looks more prestigious than one with the state attorney general, a federal judge is more prestigious than a state one, and a big-city prosecutor usually ranks higher than a small-town one. Landing a good supervisor who will actually train you and provide advice and a reference boosts the quality of any job and can be a tipping point. If you are confident you will have a better experience or gain better skills and connections in one office, or if the location fits into a broader plan, it might be worth ignoring prestige.

Geography can also play a crucial role in your decision making. If you want to practice in Denver and you are offered a summer job at the county prosecutor's office in Denver or with the U.S. Attorney's Office in South Carolina, you are usually better off going to Denver. When you apply for your 2L summer job in Denver, you will have already established that you have some ties to and interest in the region. Money can also be a geographic consideration. Some students choose a location because they have relatives or friends they can stay with; others avoid a particular city because of the high cost of living. These are things to consider before accepting an offer for an unpaid internship. Picking between a low-paying, low-prestige job and an unpaid internship can be particularly difficult. While there is something prestigious simply in getting paid, working for a solo practitioner bankruptcy attorney for $10 an hour just does not look as good on your résumé as interning for a federal court of appeals judge. If faced with one of these decisions, ask yourself how badly you need the money and if you know what you want to do next or after law school. If you are hoping to land a job with a big law firm and think you have a shot, go with the more prestigious choice. But if you think you want to practice that particular kind of law, especially if you want to practice it in that location, then the low-paying, low-prestige job should win. If you do not know what you want to do, though, err on the side of the more prestigious choice, as it will open more doors.

Interviews

I provide general advice for job interviews later in my discussion of 2L callback interviews. You can find lots of general interview advice on the Web and through your career services office, but I will offer some specific advice on telephone interviews here. If you are applying broadly for unpaid 1L jobs, possibly in other states, you might be able to avoid the cost of travel.

The same advice concerning research and preparation outlined elsewhere in this chapter applies to telephone interviews, but a little extra preparation is required. Make sure you set a firm time for the interview so you can get to a location that is quiet and, if you are using your cell phone, that has good signal. Make sure you do not have any distractions around you, such as an open computer screen showing a chat with your friends, and get out your résumé as well as any notes or prepared responses, so you have easy access to them during the interview. Because the other person cannot read your body language, it is important to convey enthusiasm in your voice. Make sure you physically smile while talking (it will show through in your voice), and consider standing up during the interview to keep your energy level high.

What to Expect at the Job

Most summer jobs you are looking for will be 40-hour-per-week positions that last somewhere from eight to twelve weeks. Some jobs involve fewer hours, though, and sometimes it is possible to split your summer by spending part of it with one employer and part with another. The exact role and responsibilities of your summer job will vary significantly based on where you are working. In a busy local prosecutor's office, you might find yourself thrown into court on easy matters. Working in a big law firm, your responsibilities will likely involve researching and assisting others on small parts of larger projects as well as a variety of training and development opportunities. You can also expect to work more hours. Small law firms might be more informal and give you more client contact.

I spent my 1L summer in a U.S. attorney's office. It was a small office with only four attorneys, not particularly busy, and I was the only summer intern. My initial projects mostly involved researching issues or subissues for the attorneys. Sometimes I simply provided them with the relevant case law (with the helpful sections highlighted); other times I prepared a very simple memo to make drafting a portion of a brief or motion easier for the attorney. Over time, I was given slightly more substantive assignments, such as drafting sentencing memos, motions, small briefs, and more meaningful memos to the Department of Justice in Washington, D.C. Eventually, I worked with an attorney on writing an appellate brief. While doing substantive work is common for those interning in a prosecutor's office, the nature and level of that work can also depend on how well you prove yourself. Do not let your lack of legal skills trouble you. Your summer employer knows that you only have a year of law school behind you, and your initial assignments will reflect this. The best way to prepare for your summer job, other than the doing the assignments in your legal writing class, is to get good at using Westlaw and LexisNexis. Keep your eyes out for the training seminars put on by the Westlaw and LexisNexis reps at your school and attend every one of them that you can. Great research skills will always leave you something to fall back on.

Try to make the most of your first summer law job by learning and developing actual skills. Volunteer for specific projects and try to take on more as the summer goes along. It is also a great opportunity to identify weaknesses and work to improve them. You should be open to and welcome constructive criticism on anything, particularly your writing—it is the way to get better. If possible, try to work closely with one or two attorneys so you will have a reference for future jobs.

What to Do If You Waited to Apply

If you are reading this section in late March or April and worrying because I advise starting the application process in the fall, do not freak out. Most of my advice still holds true for you—you want to start by prepping your documents and researching potential employers—but you are going to have to work more intensely. Depending on your circumstances, paid employment might be out. Put your energy into targeting employers that hire later in the season.

Your best bet for last-minute job applications are your school, small law firms without defined hiring programs, solo practitioners looking for unpaid interns, or smaller state trial courts. Apply broadly to these. You might have more luck landing a 20-hour-per-week position instead of a 40-hour-per-week position with someone who had not planned on hiring a summer intern, because he or she might not have a full workload for you. Most importantly, do not despair. If you keep trying, you should be able to find something. And whatever you get, as long as it shows that you gained worthwhile experience, will look good when you apply for your 2L jobs.

Key Points

- Your goals are to land a job someplace where law is practiced, develop a writing sample at that job, and end up with something interesting to talk about with prospective employers during your 2L interviews.
- Take advantage of your school's career services office, but recognize its limits.
- Keep your résumé in chronological order, emphasize your strengths, and highlight skills from past jobs that line up with some lawyer tasks (such as writing and researching).
- Make sure your résumé is professional. Do not use informal or silly e-mail addresses—use one with, perhaps, your first initial and last name as a username (e.g., jmiller@yourlawschool.edu)—and make sure that the résumé document file name has your name and nothing else.
- Most customization for individual openings should come from the cover letter.
- You may need to develop more than one résumé to fit certain employers or employer locations.
- You likely will have to work for free—a necessary sacrifice to be able to work for pay the following summer and in future years. It is better to take an unpaid legal job than a paid job unrelated to the law.
- Summer study-abroad programs are a good idea only for the student who has no intention of actively being an attorney or who is going to law school for the purpose of broadening his or her horizons, not for the student looking to gain legal experience and a job in the future.

- Unless you are sure about working in a particular market in a particular area, choose the more prestigious option you are offered regardless of location or pay. This will broaden your opportunities later and look much better on a résumé.

- When interviewing over the phone, find a quiet place to talk uninterrupted and eliminate all distractions. Convey enthusiasm and pleasantness in your tone.

- If you wait until spring to apply, your options are more limited but still exist. You may need to accept part-time unpaid jobs or search more heavily for on-campus jobs.

Chapter 15

THE 2L JOB SEARCH

FOR MANY ATTORNEYS, THE 2L JOB SEARCH IS THE MOST IMPORTANT of their careers. The big law firms recruit 2Ls to work as summer associates for the following season with the assumption that, if all goes well, they will make offers to those students for permanent employment. This practice has trickled down into some smaller firms and possibly into some government hiring. Even if you are looking at jobs after graduation that do not use a summer-associate model, your 2L job will be the top item on your résumé when you apply for a postgraduation position as a 3L, whether it is a judicial clerkship or an entry level prosecutor job.

There is no easy way to say this, but the biggest gap between the experience of attending a prestigious national law school and a local law school is seen in the 2L hiring process. In a recent ad for an in-house counsel position, Shell made explicit what others often talked about—students from tier I schools (*U.S. News and World Report*'s top fifty) must have graduated in the top 40 percent to be considered; students from tier II schools (51–100) must be in the top 25 percent; tier III students, in the top 10 percent; and tier IV students, in the top 5 percent. This hierarchy trickles down into the premier part of the 2L hiring process, on-campus interviews (OCI), in which the big national and regional firms come to law schools to recruit.

At the top schools, all students may participate in OCI. At midrange schools, employers can prescreen applicants; a typical big law firm seeks a top-10-percent class ranking (journal membership is also desired), the most prestigious firms look for the top 5 percent, and regional firms look for the top quarter. At schools a step below that, only the higher-ranked segment of the class is even invited to OCI. And at the lowest-ranked schools, only the top few, or possibly none of the students, can do OCI. If you are invited to participate in OCI and are interested in working at the law firms or government agencies that participate, try it. If it fails, then try elsewhere. If your school collects résumés, mind the deadlines and get yours in. If you are not invited to OCI or nobody comes to your campus to interview, you should try other ways to find employment, unless you are particularly courageous.

One student I know had high grades but attended a law school that no firms visited. Hundreds of law firms, however, came to recruit at the big neighboring school. After getting some basic scheduling information from a student at the big law school, she popped in to visit the recruiters during their breaks from interviewing students at the big school, shake their hands, introduce herself, and give them a résumé. This bold strategy paid off; she spent her 2L summer with that firm and now works there as an associate. Most people excluded from OCI, though, simply try other paths.

OCI: On-Campus Interviews

OCI is a series of short, 20- to 30-minute screening interviews in which big or midsized law firms and a few prestigious government employers meet 2Ls (and sometimes 3Ls). If all goes well at the on-campus interview, the law firm will invite you to visit their office for a callback interview; if that goes well, you will receive an offer to spend a summer with them; and if that summer employment goes well, you will have a job after graduation. The difference between national law schools and regional ones is seen not only in which students can participate in OCI but in the number of law firms that participate and the style of OCI.

The whole process starts months before OCI when you prepare your résumé. If you made a good résumé for your 1L job hunt, this will largely consist of updating it to reflect your 1L job and any academic honors, extracurricular leadership posts, or journal memberships collected at the end of your first year. In representing your 1L summer job, focus on what you actually did in that position and try to make it look interesting. To the extent possible, it is best to keep your OCI résumé to one page; the second page might not even get noticed as the interviewers look through scores of résumés. You should also secure a reference from one of the attorneys you worked for that summer, in case the next firm requires it.

Most employers will expect you to have a writing sample available at their request, so plan for this ahead of time. It may be perfectly appropriate to use a brief or memo from your first-year legal writing class. If you opt for this, try to improve the brief by taking into account your professor's feedback or comments on the final version. No matter the circumstances, make sure you give it one final proofread. Writing samples developed over your 1L summer can make for better writing samples. Theoretically, you should be getting better at legal writing, so this later writing will better show off your skills as of the time of the interview. Furthermore, a practical legal writing sample will have the real-world edge that class assignments do not. If the firm requests something specific (e.g., something written only for a class or only for a job), try to accommodate them. If they ask you for a writing sample (whether in person, over e-mail, or on the phone), ask them what kind of writing sample they want.

You will need permission from your employer to use something written for your job as your writing sample and will have to delete any client names or confidential details, and this process could take some time because of confidentiality concerns and red tape. The best writing sample is something persuasive, practical, written exclusively by you, and about ten pages long.

Take advantage of your school's career services office by having them review your résumé. As always, be mindful of deadlines, as career services might have a cut-off point for résumé review to manage their workflow. You should also go to all seminars, orientations, or programs put on by your school to prepare you for OCI. These will often stress the importance of doing research on the firm and tell you when you will learn details such as who is coming to interview. Make sure you visit the law firm's Web site and entry in the NALP Directory to see where it has offices, what kind of practice groups it has, and any information provided about the firm culture or summer program. Talk to 3Ls who spent their summer with that firm last year, and talk to the 2Ls who interview before you to find out what the questioners are like. You may learn who is interviewing you as late as the day of the interview, but plan to at least look the interviewers up on the firm Web site and take note of where they went to school, their practice area, and anything else that seems pertinent. If the employer is a large one, try running a Google News search or a search in the news databases on Westlaw and LexisNexis to see what is going on. This information will help you in your conversation and can also make you less nervous. Similarly, doing practice interviews or going over practice questions on your own time might make you feel more comfortable. The most important part of the interview is making a good impression and making it clear that you have an interest in that firm and that firm's location.

Some law firms host receptions at a restaurant or bar near the law school during the OCI process. If one of the firms you are interviewing with has a reception, go to it, be social, and talk to all of the attorneys there. Enjoy yourself, but obviously do not get drunk. More commonly, firms will have a hospitality suite or room at the OCI location at big schools, stocked with cookies, water, and law firm swag. Once again, try to make an appearance. Occasionally, a firm will invite the day's interviewees out to dinner in the evening—at least those to whom they intend to offer a callback interview.

Callback Interviews

If you receive a callback from the law firm, this is a great sign—half the battle is already won. A callback is a long interview at a law firm that typically involves a half-day of interviews and a lunch but can range up to a whole day. The meal is a part of the interview process, so don't treat it as something that you can skip if pressed for time. If your trip involves an overnight stay, you may also be invited out to dinner with a small group of attorneys. The costs of your travel and meal are typically covered by the law firm. Listen to your school's protocol, advice, and customs about splitting callbacks, handling travel, and so on. Do not arrive too early (waiting around for more than ten minutes is awkward) and be nice to everyone you meet. Err on the side of overdressing; wearing a suit to a business-casual office probably will not hurt your chances. It is usually a good idea to bring copies of your writing sample, résumé, transcript, and reference list with you to the interview. I always liked to bring a notepad or portfolio with me, not so much to take actual notes but to hold as a kind of legal safety blanket.

At a callback, you interview with a series of people for about thirty minutes each. You will likely interview with a mix of partners and associates, all of whom will provide feedback on you. And while they will probably all ask you the same questions, try to remember that each interviewer did not hear your answer to the previous ones. Instead of getting frustrated at this, use it as an opportunity to improve your answers.

Should you be concerned or nervous about the dining experience, see if your school offers any programs or lessons on dining manners or spend some time reading up on them online. Having made the first, big cut, you are fortunate to receive a callback, but take it seriously and prepare. The law firm will give you a list of the people you are interviewing with, so research them as you did before, but be ready to ask more questions and keep the conversation going one-on-one for the whole half-hour. Be prepared for interviewers who are less than fully prepared. Hopefully they will have reviewed your résumé and made notes, but keep in mind that these are practicing attorneys who are quite busy.

As with all interviews you face in law school, be prepared to answer standard questions such as why you went to law school, why you want to work for that employer, and what type of law you want to practice. Always listen to what the interviewer is asking and keep your answers brief, realistic (don't say that your greatest weakness is working too hard), and responsive to the interviewer's question, and avoid slang, unprofessional demeanor (limit the number of times you say "like" and try to avoid starting sentences with "so"), and jokes that are not funny. Be ready to answer a generic "tell me about yourself" question by highlighting your best points and to talk about anything on your résumé. Write out a list of questions you want to ask the employer ahead of time and have a few of them memorized in case the interviewer asks what questions you have. Simply put, you want to sound intelligent, so ask questions about the firm's mentoring and training programs, partnership track, and evaluation programs. The conventional wisdom is not to talk about the hours worked or the work-life balance in the firm as you will make yourself sound like a slacker. Also ask the hiring attorney about the firm's timing so you know when to expect to hear back. If you do not hear anything back within the timeframe they give you, a polite e-mail or phone call is appropriate.

Thank-you letters should be mailed or e-mailed as soon as possible after interview. If you send a physical note, you can mail it to the person who acted as the host or the most important person (head of a department). If you send an e-mail, you should send one to everybody you interviewed with.

If you receive an offer, you should be considerate of the law firm and other students and not delay unnecessarily in responding to it. The NALP sets guidelines governing this process (these guidelines may continue to evolve based on economic realities), and you should try to respect the rules.

Getting the Offer

If you land a summer-associate position at a big law firm during your 2L summer, your mission over the course of the summer is to receive an offer for a permanent position with the firm and to find out if you'd like to work for them.

A summer-associate position is effectively a well-paid summer-long interview. Getting an offer from your 2L summer firm is critical because, even if you do not want to work there after graduation, you will be asked by others you interview with whether or not you received an offer. The idea is that they had two to four months to get to know you at that firm, and they were able to learn more about you than than your interviewer will be able to in twenty minutes.

Not getting an offer has meant, to some, that there is something wrong with you. By the same token, getting an offer can have a positive effect—if somebody wants to take you to the prom, it must mean that you are pretty. Never underestimate the ability of lawyers to act like high schoolers. However, all of this may be changing in the wake of the Great Recession. The absence of offers may now say more about the firm than about you, and law firms may be less likely to give offers by default in the future. But, as a general rule, you should try hard to get that offer. The basic formula is quite simple: Do a good job and do not make a fool of yourself. I offer a quick dose of advice here that may be particularly helpful to readers who are nervous about their upcoming summer or lack a professional background. I also suggest looking for any programs that your school might offer that could be more in-depth.

Take your work seriously and perform it well. Try to do a good job working with different partners. Follow up with the partners you have worked for until you have enough of a track record that they can offer positive comments about you when hiring decisions are made. Take advantage of the associates and other summers. Before bugging a partner with a question, see if an associate can answer it for you first. They will often have easy answers to some of your questions and can point you toward samples and past examples of the kind of work you are trying to put together.

As for not making a fool of yourself, if you are concerned about dinner etiquette or things such as how to dress, work on this before starting the job. Read online about which fork to use or attend a program on etiquette, and ask your career services or classmates questions about dress code (also consider checking out *www.corporette.com*, a fashion blog for female professionals). If you get a chance, try to make a mental note during your interview of how people dress in the office for future reference.

One of the most common pieces of advice given to summer associates and new attorneys is to be nice to the staff—in particular, the secretaries. They tend to be permanent parts of the law firm. If you are rude, it will get around. The rest of the basic advice is pretty simple: Avoid inappropriate office relationships, watch your alcohol consumption at company events, protect client confidentiality, do not do anything to get a virus on your computer or egregiously breach computer security rules, and observe basic office etiquette. The immensely popular legal gossip blog AboveTheLaw.com runs a feature every summer with wild, embarrassing stories about 2L summer associates. Above all else, do not make AboveTheLaw.com.

The Non-OCI 2L Job Search

If you are not invited to OCI, you struck out at OCI, or you simply are not interested in OCI, you can still find summer employment. Many positions are filled outside of the OCI process, but these tend to hire later in the academic year. Jobs with small to midsize law firms, public-interest groups, and the government are usually found outside OCI. With OCI, my advice is relatively simple—do your homework and do not screw up the interview—but the process outside of OCI requires more work. At the very least, it requires you to spend more time researching potential jobs and developing a list, which once again requires you to strike a difficult balance between study time and career advancement. Pull together a list of jobs from your school, your personal network, bar association Web sites, the NALP Directory, and government Web sites. Many government agencies, such as the Department of Justice (DOJ) or the military's judge advocate general program, hire paid 2L summer interns, but to find these jobs you may have to do your own research. PSLawNet (*www.PSlawnet.org*) provides a listing of public-interest summer jobs. You should apply broadly and follow the same advice laid out in Chapter 14.

What If You Waited or Struck Out?

The best ways to find last-minute 2L jobs are to look at small law firms, some local governments, and universities, and to use family connections. Make sure you find something to continue developing experience; work for free if necessary. It is still possible to break into a big law firm after graduation—if that is your goal—as they do some recruiting of 3Ls and graduates. You can also get into a big law firm via a postgraduation judicial clerkship, which is what I did.

Key Points

- The biggest gap between the experiences of attending prestigious national law schools and local law schools is seen in the 2L hiring process.

- Do all the basics: Complete and update your résumé and cover letters, attend OCI if you are invited and the employers attending interest you, and be mindful of deadlines, especially if your school collects résumés to send them out for you.

- If you are not invited to OCI, you can try other paths to a summer job. If you go to a school where no employers visit to interview students but a neighboring school has OCI, you might be able to get in to the neighboring school to chat with the interviewers successfully.

- Secure a reference from an attorney you worked for in the previous summer in case the next firm requires it.

- Have a writing sample available in case the potential employer requests one.

- The best writing samples to use are from a 1L summer employment at a law firm or government agency, as long as the previous employer grants permission and all names and confidential information are removed.

- At law firm–sponsored receptions or parties, enjoy yourself, but do not get drunk.

- Listen to your school's protocol, advice, and customs related to callbacks.

- Research the list of interviewers you are given to learn more about who you will meet with in an interview.

- Mail thank-you letters or notes as soon as possible after the interview.

- If you receive an offer, be considerate of the firm and the other students and respond promptly in respect of the NALP guidelines.

- If you get a summer-associate position at a big law firm during the 2L summer, your goal should be to secure an offer for permanent employment by the end of your summer tenure, even if you do not end up ultimately choosing to work there.

Chapter 16

THE JUDICIAL CLERKSHIP MAZE

CLERKING FOR A JUDGE IMMEDIATELY AFTER LAW SCHOOL is one of the most prestigious jobs available to a young lawyer. Law clerks typically assist judges by preparing bench memos and drafting opinions. At the highest levels—such as the United States Supreme Court or Court of Appeals—the job involves mostly writing and editing. In other places, such as rural state courts, law clerks may have more administrative functions as well. Clerkships usually last one to two years.

There are many reasons that these positions are coveted. The experience helps new lawyers to improve both their writing skills and their understanding of judicial decision making. Exposure to good lawyering and bad lawyering, and learning how court staff distinguish between the two, helps law clerks if they later enter private practice. At higher levels, the prestige of the position can be one of the major draws. Judicial clerkships, particularly with federal judges, open up doors into some of the country's biggest firms and most elite government jobs (such the Bristow Fellowship or Department of Justice Honors Program). Some large law firms even offer signing bonuses of $50,000 to federal clerks. A prestigious clerkship is very common among candidates for law professor jobs.

One of my professors used to say that there is a clerkship for everyone. While not everyone can land a clerkship with the Supreme Court, there are many different judges at different levels. Supreme Court clerks are typically the most elite students from the most elite law schools who apply after receiving a prestigious federal circuit clerkship. Federal circuit clerks tend to have very high grades and come from the top half of their class at the very top law schools, the top 10 to 15 percent at very good schools, or at or near the actual top of their class at other schools. Many have impressive summer work experience and are members of the law review. Federal district court clerks tend to be one deviation lower in terms of grades, and the trend continues into other courts.

The selectivity of judges also depends on whether they are senior or active (senior judges being slightly less selective, although this distinction might matter more at the circuit level), the length of the term (one-year federal district court clerkships are more competitive than two-year clerkships), and where the court is located (federal courts in big cities or anywhere in California can be very competitive). Certain locations are particularly competitive; it's no easier to land a clerkship with the Southern District of New York than with a federal court of appeals. Similarly, not all state supreme courts are equally competitive—the Texas Supreme Court might be as difficult to land as a federal district court in Texas and might even be more prestigious if you plan on practicing in Texas, although the prestige is not transferable to other states in the way that federal clerkship prestige is. A student who might not be competitive for a federal clerkship might be a great fit for a state court of appeals or a state trial court.

Timing and Process

The clerkship hiring process and the timing of applications to state trial courts vary significantly. Some courts may have a formal process for hiring term clerks; others may treat the position as a normal permanent job. I suggest talking to your career services department about local judicial clerkships to find out what the process is. It's also worth checking the Web site of the county or state court system you're interested in, as these jobs may be posted there along with other local government jobs. The Vermont Law School *Guide to State Judicial Clerkships*, available online or (hopefully) through your school's career services office, provides some information on state trial court clerkships. The *Vermont Guide* is best known for its details on state supreme court clerkships, including the nuts and bolts of applying, timeframes, and salary details. This document is worth consulting, especially if you are interested in applying in multiple states.

Obviously there is a vast difference in hiring practices between federal magistrate judges and the Justices of the Supreme Court. Federal clerks typically start working in August. Most federal judges follow the Federal Law Clerk Hiring Plan, which regulates the details of the process to some extent. Under this plan, students apply at the start of their 3L years for jobs that begin after they graduate. A few days later, at a set time, judges are permitted to call students to schedule interviews that cannot be held prior to a date a few days after the call. Most court of appeals judges hire their law clerks on the first day of interviews. The actual dates vary a little each year, so it's worth Googling the key dates for the year you're interested in. Law school graduates are not held to the same rules and can apply before students. Usually it makes sense to start applying for jobs with federal court of appeals judges around May of the year before the clerkship would begin.

District judges, even those that follow the federal hiring plan, vary significantly in the hiring practices. Some interview on the first day or the days after the first day, while others may make decisions months after the hiring plan deadlines. In general, district and magistrate judges are more likely to hire later and less likely to make exploding offers (offers that must be accepted or rejected on the spot) than circuit judges, although it seems that district courts are less willing to wait to interview these days. Most federal judges use the Online System for Clerkship Application and Review (OSCAR). OSCAR is a one-stop system that provides judges with all your application materials—cover letter, transcripts, writing sample, résumé, and letters of recommendation. Judges can also use the system to provide more detail on what they want in an applicant (law review or journal membership, top 10 percent or top half of the class, and so on) as well as the kind of writing samples they want and whether they want undergraduate transcripts. A couple of judges also request LSAT scores, though they are a very tiny minority.

Aspiring Supreme Court clerks mail their applications between March and June of the year before they want to clerk. It's acceptable to apply in the spring and send a follow-up packet with your last semester's grades. As you would expect, Supreme Court clerks tend to have the best grades and extracurricular activities and recommendations from the best law schools. Most Supreme Court clerks come to the court after clerking for one of a handful of prestigious feeder judges—federal circuit judges whose clerks have previously gone on to clerk for the Supreme Court. If you really want to clerk for the Supreme Court, the first step is to identify the potential feeder judges by Googling them or asking your professors and apply for clerkships with them.

Getting Your Materials Together

It's important to get your application materials together early because it will help you avoid stress around the deadlines, ensure you meet those deadlines, and provide time for revisions and feedback from others. You should ask professors to write letters of recommendation during the second semester of your 2L year and provide them with supporting materials at their request. It's common for professors to ask for a résumé and transcript to help them craft an effective letter. A minority of professors may ask you to write a "rough draft" of a letter for them to sign. Some students are uncomfortable with this kind of assignment as it's difficult and presumptuous to write a glowing letter about yourself. Get over it. If the professor gives you the unfortunate task of writing your own letter, you really have no choice but to try to make it work. Just be honest, positive, and detailed. Stress the things that you want a judge to notice about you.

If you're applying for federal clerkships in the OSCAR system, keep your résumé to one page if it's at all possible. And it is possible. Keep in mind that federal judges receive hundreds of applications for a handful of spots. Some have their current law clerks screen the potential applicants. Most applicants will only use a one-page résumé, so clerks might not even notice that you have a second page when they view your résumé online. Anything you want them to know about you—anything you need to make it past the initial cut—should be on the first page. It's also customary to include interests on your clerkship résumé. Every candidate applying with your judge probably has impressive credentials, and judges are looking for people who are a good fit. They also provide a conversation starter for the interview. Be honest with your interests—don't tell the judge you like golf if you've never played—but try not to sound too weird or too intense.

Cover letters provide you with an opportunity to explain your local ties. If your résumé shows you working and going to school in New York and California but you're applying with a judge in Cleveland, this is a great place let the judge know that you went to high school in the suburbs of Cleveland. It's also an opportunity to explain your interest in a place that you have no ties to—why you want to work in Denver even though you've never lived in Colorado. You can also use a cover letter to try to explain away a weakness ("I have poor undergrad grades because . . ."), but this might also draw unnecessary attention to that weakness.

Selecting the ideal writing sample can be difficult, especially if you have few to choose from. The generic advice is to use an academic writing sample (a seminar paper or law review note) for appellate judges and a practical writing sample (a brief, memo, motion, and so on) for trial court judges. You should plan on using your best legal writing sample, whatever it is, unless the judge has specific parameters. Try to keep your sample in the 10-to-15-page range, which might require you to use a selection from a larger work. If you do use an excerpt, explain this at the top of the writing sample. Be sure to proofread the sample before using it and reread it before any interview. You should prepare for an interview using strategies similar to those discussed earlier in this chapter. You should also research both the judge and his or her opinions. If the judge authored big, notable opinions, read them. And even if nothing jumps out, read a few opinions so you have an idea of the judge's attitude and style. Try to find online whatever personal information you can about the judge's hobbies, activities, or interests, too.

General Advice

The best piece of advice on applying for judicial clerkships is to apply broadly. Given the prestige and difficulty of obtaining one, this is not the kind of job where you can apply to one or two positions and expect it to work out. I applied with about 120 judges; many students apply with more than that. The OSCAR system makes it particularly easy to apply with a large number of federal judges. As a basic rule, apply to any place you would be willing to work. Even if you're an excellent candidate, you should still apply broadly.

I thought that because my credentials matched what was required of clerks at the level I was applying to, I would receive lots of interviews. I also applied to a number of lower courts as backups, figuring that I could simply decline their interviews. But I received only a manageable number of interview requests because of what I call the Goldilocks situation. You see, there's only a narrow band of judges for whom you're just right. Judges for whom your credentials aren't good enough won't call, and judges for whom you're more than qualified won't call either—they expect you to get snatched up by the judges for whom you're just right. Because you're looking for the judges who will see you as just right, apply broadly.

The faculty clerkship advisor at my law school offered another way to think about how competitive the clerkship process is. After apologizing for using a stereotype, she described the difference between how women and men shop for jeans. Women want to gather as much information as possible on the jeans. They look at many different pairs, in many different stores. They compare prices and styles and try on many pairs of jeans. Men buy the first pair in their size in the first store they visit. She advised students to shop like a man when it comes to accepting judicial clerkships. Don't hold on to offers or delay in responding. Decide ahead of time where you're willing to work, and accept the first offer from the first judge who fits that.

Tips on the Federal Hiring Process

The federal hiring process is all about the timing. The first day for interviews is the most important, as many judges interview then. If at all possible, do your interviews on that day. Some judges hire clerks as soon as they find ones they like and cancel later interviews, so try to schedule your top-choice interview first thing in the morning on the first day.

Some judges are willing to interview clerks via videoconferencing or telephone, which can save you a lot of money, as they don't reimburse you for travel costs, but many still want face-to-face interviews. Figuring out realistic travel schedules—where exactly you can get to after your first interview on that day—is important. Because scheduling can be such a problem, I was advised to let all incoming calls go directly to voice mail (unless the calls come from particularly prestigious numbers, such as the 202 area code for the D.C. circuit). I then checked the voice mail immediately, wrote down where the interview opportunity was, and called back quickly after I put together a basic idea of where I could go. I had interview offers in Texas, Iowa, Michigan, and Ohio for the same day. Realistically, sticking to Michigan and Ohio allowed me to get to the most locations on that critical day. I ended up receiving an offer in the morning of that first day.

Because there's always the possibility of an exploding offer from a judge—one that you're required to accept either on the spot or within a short period of time and is designed to keep you from interviewing elsewhere—it's best to decide ahead of time whether you'll accept a particular offer. It might help to discuss this over with your significant other before the interview.

Judges who do not follow the federal hiring plan are less likely to make exploding offers. A significant number of judges either do not follow the plan or cheat on it a little. At least one circuit (the tenth) generally disregards it. Your law school might not tell you this, as some law schools are such enthusiastic supporters of the federal hiring plan that they don't want to encourage their students to take advantage of the cheaters. There are a number of clerkship-focused blogs that track which judges are hiring and when. It's important to assess whether the judge you want hires early, as you could end up applying in September, after he or she hired a full class of clerks in July.

Sometimes judges who don't normally cheat on the hiring plan will cheat if prodded. When I had an interview with a judge who did cheat, I wrote to one who didn't and asked him to interview me early. One of my friends really wanted to clerk with a circuit judge but recognized that her credentials were better suited for a district court clerkship. She decided that if she followed the plan, she'd have no chance with circuit judges, so she applied early using paper applications—OSCAR will not let 3Ls apply electronically before the deadline. Her risky strategy landed her a circuit clerkship. It might not be worth the risk for you, but it is worth considering all your options and trying to identify which judges will decide before the plan allows.

Try to be as informed as possible. You can look at clerkship blog posts from prior years to find the schools a judge has hired from before. If your school (or schools in its peer group) is not on that list, you might have to sell a judge on both you and your school. If students from your school have clerked with this judge before, talk to them; they will probably be happy to help. Some schools maintain a database of their alumni's clerkships, which you should use if available. Absent such a database, your faculty might be able to put you directly in touch with the right alumni. Faculty members also might have other tips or knowledge about particular judges' likes or dislikes. Take advantage of any resources your school can offer, as your competition is doing the same thing.

Key Points

- There is a clerkship for everybody. Just because you cannot land a clerkship with the U.S. Supreme Court does not mean you cannot get good experience working for a local judge.
- Federal clerkships are prestigious and difficult to get. It takes a significant amount of planning to apply for these clerkships.
- Most federal judges hire clerks during the early part of the 3L year, but some hire the summer before.
- State courts hire at different times.

Chapter 17

BECOMING A LAWYER: PLANNING FOR THE BAR EXAM

HOW TO PASS THE BAR EXAM IS BEYOND THE SCOPE OF THIS BOOK. But you will have to make bar exam–related decisions during law school, such as deciding whether to take classes that match the bar exam's content, going through the bar exam process, taking the Multistate Professional Responsibility Exam (MPRE), signing up for bar review classes, and registering for the bar exam itself. Knowing what you're facing with the bar exam will help you make those decisions.

Subject Matter and Course Selection

Every state except Louisiana uses the Multistate Bar Examination (MBE). The MBE is a multiple-choice test taken over six hours with 200 questions on criminal law and procedure, constitutional law, torts, property, evidence, and contracts. The second day (and third, depending on the state) is an essay test, and some states also include a performance test or additional multiple-choice questions. The actual subject matter of the essay question varies. As a representative example, these are the topics tested on the Multistate Essay Exam, from which at least 26 states draw at least some questions:

- Business organizations (agency and partnership, corporations, and LLCs)
- Conflict of laws
- Constitutional law

- Contracts
- Criminal law
- Criminal procedure
- Evidence
- Family law
- Federal civil procedure
- Negotiable instruments (commercial paper)
- Property
- Secured transactions
- Torts
- Trusts and estates
- Wills

Given how many topics are on the bar exam and how important passing it is to your future career, many students wonder whether they should take classes in law school that cover the subjects on the bar exam. Studying a bar exam topic in law school makes it a lot easier to relearn the material later. I took a two-credit class on secured transactions pass/fail in law school. Studying secured transactions for the bar was a lot easier than studying commercial paper, which I had never learned anything about before prepping for the bar.

Most students are able to learn what they need to by taking bar review classes after law school and don't need to select their law school courses around the bar. In general, I recommend taking classes in law school based on what you're interested in or the kind of law you plan on practicing, or taking entirely different classes that expose you to new topics as a way to learn what kind of law you're interested in. In other words, take the classes you want to take unless you're particularly worried about the bar or do poorly on big test—then, taking bar classes might be worth it. I recommend that everyone take classes on the six subjects on the MBE as those are covered on both days of the bar exam and the MBE itself is particularly tricky. You'll cover most of those classes in your first year of law school, so all you'll have to add is criminal procedure and evidence, if they're not already required at your school.

The MPRE

The Multistate Professional Responsibility Exam (MPRE) is a 60-question multiple-choice test required by 47 states. It covers the ethical rules for lawyers and judges. The required score varies by state, as does the timing. Many states allow you to take the exam anytime after your first year in law school, although some require you take the exam in your final year of law school. While the questions are written in the same tricky style as the MBE, the exam isn't particularly hard because the raw score needed to pass isn't very high. That said, if you don't take the MPRE seriously, you can fail.

After consulting your state's requirements, try to take the MPRE well before the bar exam. It's offered three times per year (in March, November, and August). Taking it early gives you a chance to retake the exam if necessary and removes the stress of having to take it in August, a week after the July bar exam. Many students wisely choose to take the MPRE immediately after they take their school's required professional responsibility or legal ethics class. This makes a lot of sense. An even more clever idea is to take the MPRE the same semester as your professional responsibility class. Facing the MPRE two-thirds of the way through your semester will force you to study more earlier in the semester, give you a serious practice exam, and help you ace the final exam in your class. While you need to pass the MPRE, your score doesn't go on your transcript. Your grade for your professional responsibility class does.

As far as studying for the MPRE goes, make sure you answer some actual MPRE practice questions to prepare for the tricky style of the exam. Both BARBRI and Kaplan PMBR currently offer MPRE review materials free to students who have already signed up to take their bar review classes after law school. BARBRI's review class and materials are particularly popular. One of my friends offered this advice: If you are a bright student, study for the two nights just before the MPRE; if you are not as bright, study the whole week before the MPRE.

Bar Review Classes

Almost everyone takes a bar review class after law school. These classes cost a few thousand dollars, and your law school can connect you with a bar loan to cover it. Many law firms reimburse their incoming associates for bar review costs, and the really big firms have direct-billing relationships with the bar review companies so that the students never have to pay anything. I signed up to be a campus sales representative for Kaplan PMBR. After signing up a few other students for a class they were probably going to take anyway, I earned a free MBE review class. The campus sales reps often try to sign students up early because BARBRI and Kaplan PMBR let students pay a small deposit to lock in the bar review price against future increases and give students free law school study aids in the process. For students who will ultimately take the bar review classes and won't be reimbursed by a big law firm, this can be a good deal.

The bar review market is getting more competitive, which could generate great savings for law students in the future. In general, though, I recommend not cheaping out on bar review—failing isn't worth it. I didn't take a full bar review class (only a short, nine-day course on the MBE) because I was trying to save money. I purchased books online from the Emanuel Bar Prep series for the Multistate Essay Exam and Multistate Performance Test, as well as numerous used books to help me learn the substantive material. I passed, but it was a risky strategy. I knew it was risky, so I was nervous and overstudied. Had I taken a more traditional class, I would have paid more money but followed a proven strategy with built-in benchmarks, so I would have known I was making progress.

The options available for bar review will likely increase in the future. Now you have choices such as iPod-based classes, in-person classes, and a do-it-yourself "bar review in a box." Be realistic in selecting a program that will work for you. If you need discipline and can't force yourself to study on your own, take in-person classes, even if they cost you more in the short run. If you want the peace of mind of knowing that you are going with the most popular option, then stick with BARBRI.

Registering for the Bar

You should check the Web site of your state's bar to find out what requirements you face. I want to give you two quick warnings here. A few states provide a discounted rate for first-year students who register right when they start school. At the time of writing, those states include Alabama, California, Florida, Illinois, Iowa, Kentucky, Mississippi, Missouri, North Dakota, Ohio, Oklahoma, and Texas. The other thing to know is that applying to sit for the bar exam is actually a somewhat lengthy process as the character and fitness sections require you to fill out a lot of forms and assemble items such as driving records, so do not wait until the last minute to start the process.

Key Points

- You do not necessarily have to take law school classes on topics that are on the bar exam, but it might be worth doing so if you are nervous.
- You probably have to take a legal ethics exam called the Multistate Professional Responsibility Exam (MPRE) before becoming a lawyer.
- Plan on taking a bar review class, and consider signing up early to save money.

Index